Social Media Analytics and Data Analysis

Ms. Sarita Singh
Ms. Manisha Verma
Md. Shadab Hussain
Dr. Anurag Upadhyay

KAVYA PUBLICATIONS

Publisher:

SDR INNOWAYS INDIA PVT. LTD.
667, Rajaward, Kulpahar, Mahoba – 210426

Imprint:
KAVYA PUBLICATIONS
Plot No.107C, Hanuman Khand, Gulabvatika, Behta Hazipur, Loni-UP (Near Dilshad Garden Delhi) NCR -201102

Mob. : 7905266820
Website : www.kavyapublications.com
E-Mail : info@kavyapublications.com

ISBN : 978-93-6431-862-4
Price : 499 /-
Year : 2025

This book is printed at MTL and published by author Ajay Agrawal, CEO of SDR Innoways India Pvt. Ltd. Kulpahar Mahoba with its imprint and centre, Kavya Publications Delhi.

PREFACE

In today's hyper-connected world, social media is no longer just a platform for communication—it is a dynamic ecosystem of real-time human behavior, opinion, and influence. Platforms like Twitter, Instagram, TikTok, and LinkedIn generate massive volumes of data that offer unprecedented insights into trends, sentiment, public discourse, and even predictive behavior. Harnessing this data for strategic, academic, or technological purposes is the essence of Social Media Analytics and Data Analysis.

This book is designed to serve as a comprehensive guide for students, researchers, professionals, and data enthusiasts who want to understand and apply analytical methods to social media data. It brings together key concepts from data science, natural language processing, and network analysis, and applies them directly to social platforms through practical, real-world examples.

The aim is twofold:

- To demystify the process of collecting, cleaning, and analyzing social media data.
- To equip readers with tools to make informed decisions based on trends, sentiment, influence, and patterns of user behavior.

ABOUT THE AUTHORS

MS. SARITA SINGH

Sarita Singh is a research scholar in Computer Science and Engineering at Invertis University, Bareilly India, and currently serves as an Assistant Professor at KCC Institute of Technology & Management. With over **8 years of academic and research experience**, her core interests lie in **cryptography, information security**, and **machine learning**, with a strong focus on **substitution ciphers**, **secure communication frameworks**, and **cyber threat detection**.

MS. MANISHA VERMA

Ms. Manisha Verma is currently as an Assistant Professor in the Department of Computer Science at KCC Institute of Technology and Management, Greater Noida, India. She holds an M.Tech from AKTU, Lucknow, awarded in 2016. Prior to that, she earned her Master of Computer Applications from Punjab Technical University, Jalandhar, in 2010. She is presently pursuing a Ph.D. in Computer Science and Technology from Galgotias University, Greater Noida.Ms. Verma has authored multiple research publications, including patents, journal articles, and papers presented at national and international conferences.

MD. SHADAB HUSSAIN

Md. Shadab Hussain is a research scholar in Computer Science and Engineering at Invertis University and an Assistant Professor at G. L. Bajaj Institute of Technology and Management, Greater Noida. With over 15 years of academic and industry experience, his expertise spans cybersecurity, cryptography, and machine learning. He has published in reputed journals, contributed book chapters, and guided over 100 student projects.

DR. ANURAG UPADHYAY

Dr. Anurag Upadhyay ,Working as Assistant Professor at KCC Institute of Technology and Management, Greater Noida in CSE Department ,He bring 16 years of teaching experience from various Institutes. In "Social Media Analytics and Data Analysis," Dr. Anurag combines theoretical foundations with practical applications to guide students, marketers, and analysts through the complexities of extracting meaningful insights from platforms.

INDEX

UNIT-I

1.1 Introduction to Social Media

Social media refers to online platforms and tools that allow users to create, share, and interact with content and other users. These platforms enable communication, networking, entertainment, and information sharing on a global scale. Social media refers to digital platforms and technologies that enable users to create, share, and interact with content and with each other in virtual communities. Since its rise in the early 2000s, social media has transformed the way people communicate, access information, and express themselves.

1.2 Origins and Evolution of Social Media

Early social media platforms, such as MySpace and LiveJournal, were designed for people to connect with friends and family. MySpace, which allowed users to create personal profile pages and share information about themselves, became the first network to reach one million active monthly users in 2004. LiveJournal, a platform where users could share journal-like entries with either public or private networks, reached over 2.5 million active accounts in 2005.

Social media use grew rapidly in the 2000s and early 2010s as Facebook and X (formerly Twitter) became popular. Like MySpace, Facebook users create profiles to share information about themselves, while other users leave comments. Initially used for socializing among college-age users, social media became popular with younger and older users.

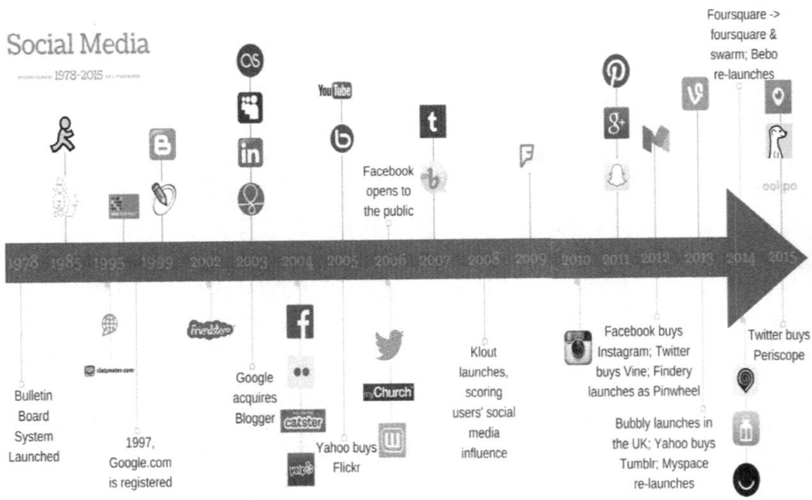

In 2006, X's launch included its feed feature, where posts from accounts that a user followed were aggregated onto a single page. Facebook launched its own News Feed feature. The news feed became a standard feature for many social media platforms. More users began posting links to external sites, where news stories, current events, and product pages could be shared with personal updates. Users could interact with each other's content, including liking, sharing, and commenting on posts.

1. **Early Foundations (1970s–1990s)**
    - **Bulletin Board Systems (BBS):** In the late 1970s and early 1980s, users accessed BBSs to share messages and files over dial-up connections.
    - **Usenet (1980):** Created as a distributed discussion system, Usenet allowed users to post public messages and comment on various topics.
    - **Internet Relay Chat (IRC) (1988):** Enabled real-time text communication among users, laying the groundwork for online chats and forums.
2. **The Birth of Social Networking (1997–2005)**
    - **SixDegrees.com (1997):** Often cited as the first recognizable social networking site. It allowed users to create profiles and list friends.
    - **Friendster (2002) and MySpace (2003):** Expanded social networking to music and entertainment communities.
    - **LinkedIn (2003):** Focused on professional networking and business connections.
    - **Facebook (2004):** Initially limited to Harvard students, it later expanded to the public and revolutionized personal social networking.
3. **Expansion and Diversification (2006–2015)**
    - **Twitter (2006):** Introduced microblogging with 140-character messages ("tweets"), emphasizing real-time communication.
    - **YouTube (2005):** Transformed video sharing and consumption.
    - **Instagram (2010) and Snapchat (2011):** Popularized visual-based content, filters, and stories.

- **Social media on mobile:** The rise of smartphones and apps significantly increased social media access and usage.

4. Dominance and Integration (2016–Present)

- **TikTok (2016):** Emerged as a major platform for short-form videos, especially among younger audiences.
- **Platform convergence:** Features like stories, live streaming, and e-commerce became standard across platforms (e.g., Facebook, Instagram, YouTube).
- **AI and algorithms:** Platforms now use sophisticated algorithms to curate content, ads, and recommendations.
- **Meta** (Facebook's parent company) and others are exploring metaverse and augmented reality as the next frontier of social interaction.

1.3 How Social Media Is Used Today

As users continued to spend more time on social media sites, different types of social media platforms evolved. They can be broadly categorized as:

- Social networks: Facebook, NextDoor
- Microblogging: X, BlueSky, Mastodon, Threads
- Long-form blogging: Substack, Ghost
- Professional networking: LinkedIn, Behance, ResearchGate
- Video and photo sharing: Instagram, TikTok, YouTube, Snapchat
- Visual curation and search: Pinterest, Houzz, DeviantArt
- Messaging: WhatsApp, Signal, WeChat, Marco Polo
- Community forums: Reddit, Discord, Clubhouse

Top 10 Global Social Media Platforms

The average social media user spends **two hours and 21 minutes** each day on social media, visiting an average of **6.8** different social media platforms each month. These were the most widely used social media providers as of February 2025, according to Data Reportal:

- Facebook (3.07 billion users)
- YouTube (2.53 billion users)
- WhatsApp (2 billion users)
- Instagram (2 billion users)
- TikTok (1.59 billion users)
- WeChat (1.38 billion users)
- Telegram (950 million users)
- Facebook Messenger (947 million users)
- Snapchat (850 million users)
- Douyin (766 million users)

The Web 2.0 Revolution and the Rise of Modern Social Media (Mid-2000s - 2010s)

The concept of Web 2.0, coined in 1999 and popularized after a 2004 conference, significantly influenced the development of social media. Web 2.0 marked a shift from static, information-driven websites (Web 1.0) to dynamic, interactive platforms that encouraged user-generated content (UGC), collaboration, and social interaction. Key aspects of Web 2.0 that fueled social media's growth include:

User Empowerment: Users transitioned from passive consumers to active participants who could create, share, and modify content.

Interactivity: Features like comments, likes, shares, and ratings fostered engagement and a sense of community.

Syndication: Technologies like RSS feeds allowed users to subscribe to and integrate content from various sources.

APIs (Application Programming Interfaces): These allowed different applications to communicate, facilitating the integration of features and data across platforms.

1.4 Social Media Landscape

The social media landscape is a dynamic and ever-evolving environment, characterized by the continued dominance of established platforms, the rise of new trends, and an increasing focus on user experience, authenticity, and emerging technologies.

The social media landscape is vast and constantly evolving. It encompasses a wide range of platforms that serve different purposes, audiences, and content types. Understanding this landscape is essential for users, creators, and businesses to effectively navigate and engage online.

1. Major Social Media Platforms (2024 Overview)

A. Meta-Owned Platforms

- Facebook – Still the largest platform (2.9B+ monthly users), strong for communities, ads, and older demographics.
- Instagram – Focus on visuals (photos, Reels, Stories), popular among Gen Z and Millennials.
- WhatsApp – Dominates messaging in many countries (2B+ users).
- Threads – Meta's Twitter competitor, growing rapidly with Instagram integration.

B. Video-Centric Platforms

- YouTube – Leading long-form video platform (2.5B+ users).
- TikTok – Short-form video king, algorithm-driven, huge Gen Z & Alpha appeal.

- Snapchat – Popular for ephemeral content, AR filters, and younger users.

C. Professional & Niche Networks

- LinkedIn – B2B networking, job hunting, and industry thought leadership.
- Reddit – Forum-based discussions (subreddits), strong for niche communities.
- Pinterest – Visual discovery, DIY, and shopping inspiration.

D. Emerging & Alternative Platforms

- X (Twitter) – Struggling with brand changes but still key for news and debates.
- Discord – Community-driven chat (gamers, crypto, fandoms).
- Bluesky – Decentralized Twitter alternative (gaining traction).
- Tumblr & Mastodon – Niche, text-heavy, and decentralized options.

2. Key Trends Shaping Social Media (2024)

A. Rise of AI & Automation

- AI-generated content (ChatGPT, DALL·E, deepfakes).
- Chatbots for customer service.
- Algorithmic personalization (TikTok's "For You Page" model spreading to other platforms).

B. Short-Form Video Dominance

- TikTok-style content expanding (Instagram Reels, YouTube Shorts).
- Vertical video as the default format.

C. Social Commerce & Shoppable Content

- In-app shopping (Instagram, TikTok Shop, Pinterest).

- Influencer-driven sales (live shopping, affiliate marketing).

D. Privacy & Decentralization

- Users demanding more control over data.
- Growth of decentralized platforms (Bluesky, Mastodon).
- Decline of traditional tracking (Apple's App Tracking Transparency).

E. Authenticity & "Anti-Perfection"

- Raw, unfiltered content (BeReal's influence).
- Decline of overly curated feeds.

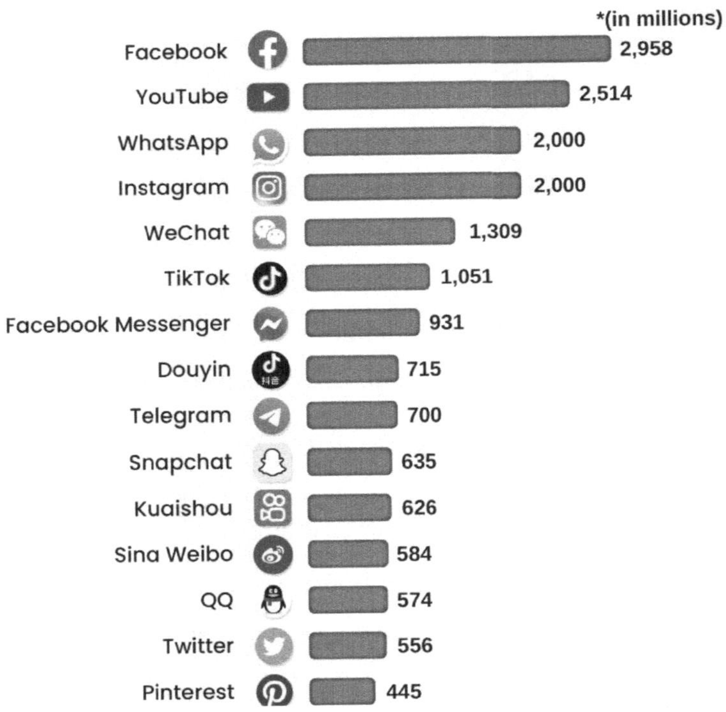

3. User Demographics & Behavior

Platform	Primary Age Group	Key Usage
Facebook	25 - 45+	Community groups, marketplace
Instagram	18-34	Visual storytelling, Reels
TikTok	13-30	Viral trends, entertainment
LinkedIn	25-55	Professional networking, B2B
X (Twitter)	18-40	News, debates, memes
Snapchat	13-25	Private messaging, AR filters

- Gen Z (1997-2012) → TikTok, Instagram, Snapchat.
- Millennials (1981-1996) → Facebook, Instagram, YouTube.
- Gen X (1965-1980) → Facebook, YouTube, LinkedIn.
- Boomers (1946-1964) → Facebook, YouTube.

1.5 Social media analytics

Social media analytics is the process of collecting data from social media networks and gaining insights in order to improve the performance of social media campaigns. Social media analytics tools perform these analysis with the use of technologies such as data mining, data analytics, and big data.

Social analytics is the key to ensure high-level performance of your social media campaigns, and also to make data-driven decisions. It helps your social media team learn what works and what does not work when it comes to content and strategy. This analysis is based on the level of audience engagement, conversion, and outreach.

For example, the number of likes on your post on Facebook defines the level of audience engagement, whereas the number of clicks on a LinkedIn post indicates conversions. Based on the likes and clicks, you can measure the performance of your content and tweak your future content strategy. Similarly, when you analyze your competitor's social networks, it gives you an idea of what content is performing better.

Social media analytics helps companies address these experiences and use them to:

- Spot trends related to offerings and brands
- Understand conversations — what is being said and how it is being received
- Derive customer sentiment towards products and services
- Gauge response to social media and other communications
- Identify high-value features for a product or service
- Uncover what competitors are saying and its effectiveness
- Map how third-party partners and channels may affect performance

Social Media Analytics steps:

Social media analytics encompasses the measurement, analysis, and interpretation of interactions on social media platforms. It involves:

- **Data Collection:** Gathering raw data such as likes, comments, shares, mentions, followers, reach, impressions, clicks, video views, and sentiment. This can be done through native platform analytics (e.g., Facebook Insights, X Analytics, Instagram Insights) or specialized third-party tools.

- **Data Analysis:** Processing and organizing this raw data to identify patterns, trends, and relationships. This often involves segmenting data by demographics, location, or other relevant factors.
- **Interpretation & Insights:** Translating the analyzed data into meaningful insights that explain past performance and inform future actions. This is where the "why" comes into play – understanding the underlying reasons for certain metrics.
- **Reporting & Visualization:** Presenting findings in clear, concise reports and dashboards that are easy to understand and act upon.

1.6 Key Metrics in Social Media Analytics:

Social media analytics typically focuses on several categories of metrics:

Awareness Metrics:

- **Reach:** The number of unique users who saw your content.

Example:

Your post was shown to 500 unique users.

Even if some users saw it multiple times, **Reach = 500**

- **Impressions:** The total number of times your content was displayed (even if the same person saw it multiple times).

Example:

Your post appears 3 times in one user's feed and 1 time in another user's feed.

Total Impressions = 3 (User A) + 1 (User B) = 4 Impressions

- **Follower Growth:** The rate at which your audience is increasing.

$$\text{Follower Growth Rate} = \left(\frac{\text{New Followers}}{\text{Total Followers at Start}}\right) \times 100$$

Example:

Start of the month: 1,000 followers

End of the month: 1,150 followers

New Followers = 150

$$\text{Follower Growth Rate} = \left(\frac{150}{1000}\right) \times 100 = 15\%$$

- **Share of Voice (SoV):** Measures how much people talk about your brand compared to your competitors.

$$\text{SoV} = \left(\frac{\text{Mentions of Your Brand}}{\text{Total Mentions in Industry}}\right) \times 100$$

Mentions of your brand: 200

Total mentions in industry: 1,000

SOV = (200/1000)*100 = 20 %

- **Brand Mentions:** How often your brand or related keywords are mentioned across platforms.

Example:

In a week, users tagged or mentioned your brand in 85 posts.

Brand Mentions = 85

Engagement Metrics:

Likes/Reactions: Positive interactions with your content.

Comments/Replies: Direct responses and discussions.

Shares/Retweets: How often your content is redistributed by others.

Engagement Rate: The percentage of your audience that interacts with your content.

Engagement Rate = (Total Engagement / Reach or Impressions)

Total Engagements = likes + comments + shares

Example:

Likes = 50, Comments = 20, Shares = 10

Reach = 1,000

$$\text{Engagement Rate} = \left(\frac{80}{1000}\right) \times 100 = 8\%$$

Click-Through Rate (CTR): The percentage of people who clicked on a link in your post.

$$\text{CTR} = \left(\frac{\text{Link Clicks}}{\text{Impressions}}\right) \times 100$$

Example:

Link Clicks = 120

Impressions = 3,000

$$\text{CTR} = \left(\frac{120}{3000}\right) \times 100 = 4\%$$

Video Views/Completion Rate: How many times your videos are watched and for how long.

$$\text{Completion Rate} = \left(\frac{\text{Completed Views}}{\text{Total Views}}\right) \times 100$$

Example:

Total Views = 600

Views that watched until the end = 180

$$\text{Completion Rate} = \left(\frac{180}{600}\right) \times 100 = 30\%$$

Conversion Metrics:

- **Conversions:** The number of desired actions taken (e.g., website visits, lead form submissions, purchases) driven by social media.

$$\text{Conversion Rate} = \left(\frac{\text{Conversions}}{\text{Clicks}}\right) \times 100$$

Example:

Conversions = 30

Clicks = 120

$$\text{Conversion Rate} = \left(\frac{30}{120}\right) \times 100 = 25\%$$

- **Return on Investment (ROI):** The financial return generated from social media efforts.

$$\text{ROI} = \left(\frac{\text{Net Profit from Social Media}}{\text{Cost of Social Media Investment}}\right) \times 100$$

Example

Revenue from a Facebook campaign = **$5,000**

Cost of the campaign = **$2,000**

$$\text{Net Profit} = \$5,000 - \$2,000 = \$3,000$$

$$\text{ROI} = \left(\frac{3000}{2000}\right) \times 100 = 150\%$$

- **Average Watch Time (Bonus Metric)-** Average duration viewers watch the video before dropping off.

Example:

Total watch time across all views = **1,800 seconds**

Total views = 600

$$\text{Average Watch Time} = \frac{1800}{600} = 3 \text{ seconds}$$

Audience Metrics:

1. **Demographics:** Information about your followers (age, gender, location, interests).
2. **Audience Activity:** When your audience is most active online.

Sentiment Metrics:

- **Sentiment Analysis:** The overall tone of conversations about your brand (positive, negative, neutral).

Example of Sentiment Analysis

Let's say you collected 1,000 social media mentions (comments, tweets, or reviews) about a product.

Raw Data (after classification):

Positive mentions: 600

Negative mentions: 250

Neutral mentions: 150

1.Sentiment Distribution (Percentage)

$$\text{Percentage} = \left(\frac{\text{Type of Mentions}}{\text{Total Mentions}}\right) \times 100$$

Calculations:

- **Positive Sentiment** = (600 / 1000) × 100 = **60%**
- **Negative Sentiment** = (250 / 1000) × 100 = **25%**
- **Neutral Sentiment** = (150 / 1000) × 100 = **15%**

Sentiment Score (Optional Metric)

One common scoring system assigns:

- +1 for positive
- 0 for neutral
- -1 for negative

$$\text{Sentiment Score} = \frac{(\text{Positive Mentions} \times 1) + (\text{Neutral} \times 0) + (\text{Negative Mentions} \times (-1))}{\text{Total Mentions}}$$

Calculation:

$$\text{Sentiment Score} = \frac{(600 \times 1) + (150 \times 0) + (250 \times -1)}{1000} = \frac{600 - 250}{1000} = 0.35$$

Sentiment Score = 0.35

(Score ranges from -1 to +1, so this reflects moderately positive sentiment.)

1.7 Social Media Analytics in Small and Large Organizations

Social Media Analytics involves collecting, analyzing, and interpreting data from social platforms (e.g., Facebook, Instagram, X/Twitter, LinkedIn) to support marketing, customer service, and brand strategy.

Social media analytics (SMA) helps businesses measure performance, understand audience behavior, and optimize marketing strategies. However, its application differs significantly between small and large organizations due to resources, goals, and scale.

Key Differences in Social Media Analytics

Small Organisations

Resource Constraints

- Limited budget for premium analytics tools
- Reliance on free or low-cost platforms (e.g., Meta Insights, Google Analytics)

- Small or no dedicated social media team

Focus Areas

- Engagement metrics (likes, shares, comments)
- Customer sentiment and direct interactions
- Lead generation and conversion tracking

Implementation Characteristics

- Manual or semi-automated reporting
- Quick, agile decision-making based on real-time data
- Strong focus on local or niche audience targeting

Challenges

- Limited data integration with other business systems
- Difficulty in benchmarking against competitors
- Less structured analytics processes

Large Organizations

Resource Availability

- Dedicated social media analytics teams
- Enterprise tools (e.g., Hootsuite, Sprinklr, Brandwatch)
- AI-powered sentiment analysis and predictive analytics

Focus Areas

- Brand reputation and crisis management
- Competitive benchmarking and market trends
- ROI measurement across multiple campaigns

Implementation Characteristics

- Automated dashboards and real-time reporting

- Cross-departmental data integration (marketing, sales, customer service)
- Advanced segmentation (demographics, psychographics, buyer journey)

Challenges

- Data overload leading to analysis paralysis
- Siloed data across different platforms
- Slower response times due to corporate approval processes

1.8 Common Social Media Analytics Techniques

Technique	Small Organizations	Large Organizations
Sentiment Analysis	Basic manual monitoring (emoji reactions, comments)	AI-driven NLP tools for brand perception tracking
Competitor Analysis	Informal comparisons (manual checks)	Automated benchmarking (Share of Voice, Share of Engagement)
ROI Tracking	Simple link tracking (UTM parameters)	Multi-touch attribution models
Audience Insights	Basic demographic data from free tools	Advanced psychographic profiling
Team size	1–3 people	Dedicated departments or agencies
Tools used	Free/low-cost tools	Advanced enterprise tools
Data depth	Basic metrics (likes, clicks)	Advanced metrics (sentiment, attribution)

Use of insights	Tactical (e.g., content tweaks)	Strategic (campaigns, brand positioning)
Budget	Very limited	Substantial, with ROI expectations
Integration with business	Often standalone	Integrated with CRM, ERP, marketing systems

1.9 Application of Social Media Analytics in Different Social Media Platforms

The application of Social Media Analytics (SMA) varies across different platforms because each offers unique features, user behaviors, and business tools. Here's a breakdown of how SMA is applied across the major social media platforms.

1. Facebook / Meta (includes Instagram)

Key Metrics:

- Engagement (likes, shares, comments)
- Reach & impressions
- Video views
- Click-through rate (CTR)
- Ad performance (cost per click, conversion rate)

Analytics Tools:

- Meta Business Suite
- Facebook Insights / Instagram Insights
- Ads Manager

Application:

- Audience analysis: Demographics, locations, behavior

- Campaign optimization: Monitor ad performance, adjust targeting
- Content strategy: Track post performance and best times to post
- Sentiment analysis: Monitor public reactions to posts, ads, or events.

2. X (formerly Twitter)

Key Metrics:

- Engagement (retweets, likes, replies)
- Impressions
- Follower growth
- Hashtag performance
- Link clicks

Analytics Tools:

- Twitter Analytics
- Third-party tools like Hootsuite, Brandwatch, Sprout Social

Application:

- Trend tracking: Monitor hashtags and real-time discussions
- Brand monitoring: Real-time listening to mentions or complaints
- Crisis management: Measure sentiment and response effectiveness
- Influencer tracking: Evaluate reach and interaction of influencer campaigns

3. LinkedIn

Key Metrics:

- Engagement (reactions, comments, shares)
- Click-throughs to website or job postings

- Follower demographics
- Post reach
- Company page views

Analytics Tools:

- LinkedIn Analytics (Company Pages)
- LinkedIn Campaign Manager (for paid ads)

Application:

- B2B marketing: Track performance of thought leadership content
- Recruitment insights: Monitor traffic and engagement on job posts
- Professional engagement: Analyze what types of posts resonate with business audiences
- Lead generation: Evaluate InMail and sponsored content effectiveness

4. YouTube

Key Metrics:

- Watch time and audience retention
- Views, likes, comments
- Subscriber growth
- Traffic sources
- Click-through rate on thumbnails

Analytics Tools:

- YouTube Studio Analytics

Application:

- Content optimization: See which videos keep viewers engaged
- SEO strategy: Analyze search terms and viewer sources

- Monetization tracking: Track revenue and ad performance
- Audience insights: Understand viewer demographics and preferences

5. TikTok

Key Metrics:

- Video views and watch time
- Likes, comments, shares
- Follower growth
- Traffic sources
- Trending sounds and hashtags

Analytics Tools:

- TikTok Pro/Business Analytics
- Third-party tools like Analisa.io

Application:

- Trend tracking: Monitor what's trending to stay relevant
- Engagement strategy: Analyze what short-form content goes viral
- Hashtag campaigns: Measure participation and reach
- Audience targeting: Identify which content resonates with different groups

1.10 Comparison Table

Platform	Primary Use Case	Key Analytics Focus	Common Tools
Facebook	Broad reach, ads, brand building	Engagement, ads, audience targeting	Meta Business Suite, Ads Manager
Instagram	Visual branding,	Stories/Posts	Instagram

	influencer work	engagement, reach, content trends	Insights
X (Twitter)	News, real-time engagement	Hashtags, mentions, sentiment	Twitter Analytics, Hootsuite
LinkedIn	B2B marketing, recruitment	Professional engagement, lead generation	LinkedIn Analytics, Campaign Manager
YouTube	Video content, monetization	Watch time, retention, SEO	YouTube Studio
TikTok	Short-form viral content	Video performance, trends, audience growth	TikTok Analytics, Analisa.io

1.11 Types of Social Networks

Social networks can be categorized based on their primary purpose, audience, and content format. Below are the main types, along with examples and key characteristics.

1. Social networks

Social networking sites help people connect with each other and offer a multitude of ways for different brands to attract individuals. Users can share their thoughts, form groups based on their interests, curate content, upload photos and videos and participate in group discussions.

You can reach wide and diverse audiences with advertisements and persuade influential people with the right targeting metrics. You can also build connections between your brand and those individuals, research user preferences and monitor online conversations about your business.

Learning what people post about your brand on social networks can help you use that information to create a positive presence and boost brand awareness.

Examples of social networking platforms:

Facebook ,Twitter ,Instagram ,LinkedIn , TikTok

2. Discussion forums

Discussion forums encourage people to answer each other's questions and share ideas and news. Many of these social media sites focus on posing questions to solicit the best answer. Answering them correctly and honestly can increase your credibility on the forum.

That credibility and respect could lead to an increase in visits to your business or product website. You can also use discussion forums to do market research by asking people what they think of your products and brand. This can help you create more focused marketing campaigns.

Examples of discussion forums:

Reddit , Digg , Quora ,Clubhouse

3. Image-sharing networks

These social media sites let people share photos and related content. They offer a platform to start conversations, inspire creativity, make products seem more appealing and encourage customers to talk about your brand.

For example, a clothing company could give everyone who posts a picture of their gear on the image-sharing network a chance to win a gift certificate.

Examples of image-sharing networks:

Instagram , Flickr , Photobucket

4. Bookmarking networks

Bookmarking networks are platforms where users save different ideas, articles, posts and other content for later use. Many people also share links to lists of online resources. The purpose of these websites is to discover new content based on shared interests and to discuss trends.

You can use these networks to direct people to your website and engage with and influence their opinion by sharing your own content to bookmark.

Examples of bookmarking networks:

Feedly , Flipboard , Pocket , StumbleUpon , Pinterest

5. Blogging and publishing networks

These social media networks give you a place to publish your thoughts on your job, current events, hobbies and more. You can enjoy many of the benefits of having your own blog without having to host it on your own website.

You can also attract new readers from the pool of people who visit the network looking for interesting content. Consider writing blog posts about how to use your product in creative ways or post news about your industry to drive more traffic to your account.

Examples of blogging and publishing networks:

Medium , WordPress , Facebook , Tumblr

6. Consumer review networks

These sites display customers' reviews of businesses, giving users a full perspective of the type of services and products offered and the overall satisfaction rate. Customer reviews can help you identify any common problems that many people share and allow you to improve their experiences over time.

Promoting positive reviews and thoughtfully handling negative ones can make your business more popular and boost brand awareness.

Examples of consumer review networks:

TripAdvisor , Yelp , OpenTable , Google My Business

7. Interest-based networks

Use these specialized networks to share your hobbies and unique interests with others. Sites and apps related to your industry can help you network by shared interest as well.

For example, an interest-based site could allow people to discuss their favorite books and get recommendations about what to read next. Authors could create profile pages to promote their work and answer questions from readers.

Examples of interest-based networks:

Strava , Peanut , Goodreads

8. Sharing economy networks

These sites give people access to resources by encouraging them to share goods and services. For example, a sharing economy site focused on pets could help a user find someone willing to take care of their dog while on vacation.

It would be less costly than a kennel and more comfortable for the pet. If your company sells pet toys or food, you could gain new customers by advertising, perhaps by offering promotions of your products or services for users to try. '

Examples of sharing economy networks:

Lending Club , Couchsurfing , Eatwith

9. Social shopping networks

These networks help people spot trends, share great finds, make purchases and follow their favorite brands. They focus on e-commerce, and the social element makes it engaging and entertaining. These social shopping sites are ideal for building awareness about your brand and selling to a wider audience.

Many of them let hobbyists and small business owners sell their art, jewelry, crafts and other items. Sellers are able to reach customers who are looking for unique, handmade products. Other social shopping networks offer home-related products along with content about home improvement, making them interest-based networks as well. Many social networks now also include social shopping elements. People can sell items to their friends, followers and other buyers near them, making it much easier to get rid of old appliances and furniture.

Examples of social shopping networks:

Instagram , Poshmark , Etsy , Facebook

10. Video hosting platforms

Video hosting platforms give independent filmmakers, journalists and other creators a way for their audiences to stream videos quickly and easily. Brands can use paid ads to reach new customers, they can ask influencers to use and talk about their products or they can film their own video content.

Examples of video hosting platforms:

YouTube, TikTok , Snapchat , Vimeo , Instagram

Type	Purpose	Examples
Social Connection	Personal interaction	Facebook, Instagram, Snapchat
Professional Networking	Careers and business	LinkedIn, XING
Media Sharing	Share videos, images	YouTube, TikTok, Pinterest
Discussion/Forum	Conversations and Q&A	Reddit, Quora

Consumer Reviews	Rate and review services/products	Yelp, TripAdvisor
Blogging/Publishing	Long-form content creation	Medium, WordPress
Interest-Based	Communities for shared passions	Goodreads, Strava
Private/Anonymous	Encrypted or identity-free sharing	Discord, Telegram

1.12 Friend, user-generated content of Social Media Analytics

In Social Media Analytics (SMA), the terms “friend” and “user-generated content ” represent important data points and social interactions that businesses analyze to understand user behavior, brand engagement, and community dynamics.

1. Friend (or Follower/Connection) in Social Media Analytics

Definition:

A friend is a person with whom a user has a mutual connection on social media. On different platforms, this may be called a follower, subscriber, or connection (e.g., LinkedIn, Twitter, Instagram).

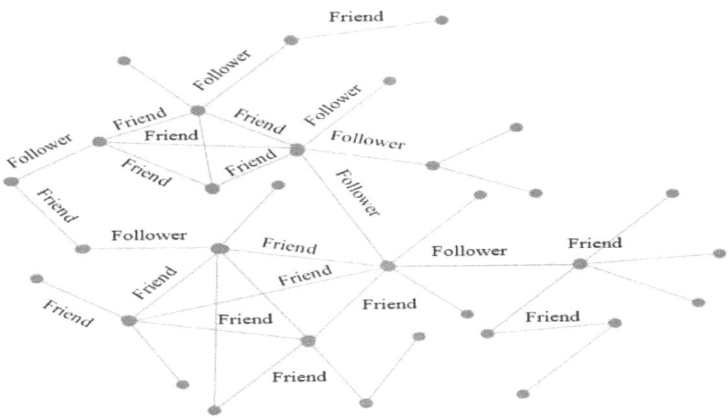

Analytics Application:

Metric	Purpose
Friend/Follower count	Measures reach and audience growth
Follower demographics	Understand audience profile (age, gender, location)
Follower growth rate	Tracks performance of campaigns in attracting followers
Influencer connections	Analyze network influence and social reach
Churn rate (unfollows)	Identify loss of interest or poor content performance

2. User-Generated Content (UGC)

Definition:

UGC refers to any content created and shared by users, not the brand itself. This includes:

Photos, videos, reviews, stories

Comments, memes, testimonials

Hashtag campaigns or challenges

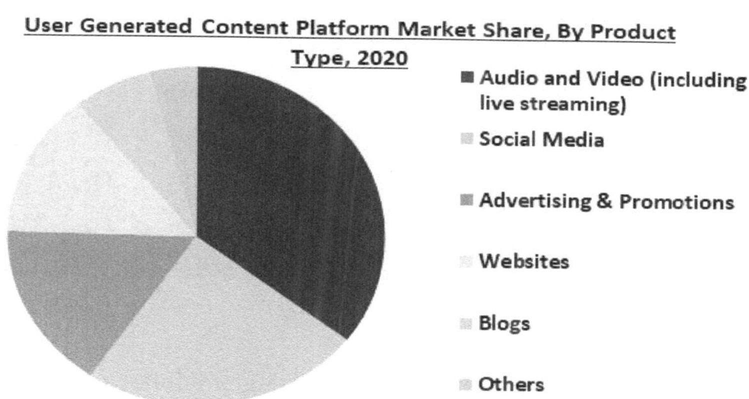

Analytics Application:

Metric or Focus	Purpose
Volume of UGC	Measures audience participation and brand engagement
Engagement on UGC	Tracks likes, shares, and comments on user-created content
Sentiment analysis	Understand emotional tone in user posts
Hashtag tracking	Identify content under branded or viral hashtags
Content virality	Assess how far and fast user content spreads

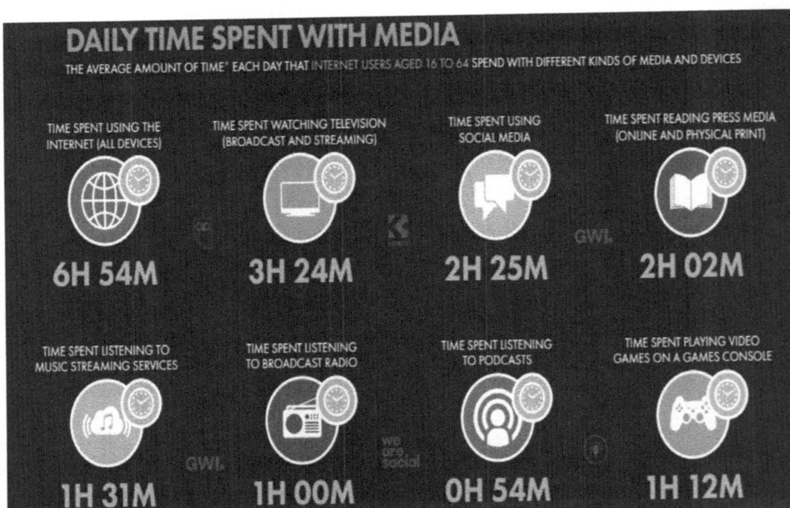

Numerical Problem:

A company is tracking its Instagram follower metrics a 3-month campaign period.

- Starting followers (Month 0): 10,000
- Followers at end of Month 1: 11,200
- Followers at end of Month 2: 12,000
- Followers at end of Month 3: 12,600
- Unfollows over 3 months: 800 total
- New followers over 3 months: 3,400 total

1. **Follower Growth Rate**

$$\text{Growth Rate (\%)} = \left(\frac{\text{New Followers}}{\text{Starting Followers}}\right) \times 100$$

$$\text{Growth Rate} = \left(\frac{3,400}{10,000}\right) \times 100 = 34\%$$

Result: Follower base grew by 34% over 3 months.

2. **Average Monthly Follower Growth**

$$\text{Average Monthly Growth} = \frac{\text{Total New Followers}}{3} = \frac{3,400}{3} \approx 1,133 \text{ followers/month}$$

Result: Gaining ~1,133 new followers per month on average.

3. **Follower Churn Rate (Unfollows Rate)**

$$\text{Churn Rate (\%)} = \left(\frac{\text{Unfollows}}{\text{Total Followers Gained}}\right) \times 100 = \left(\frac{800}{3,400+800}\right) \times 100 = \left(\frac{800}{4,200}\right) \times 100 \approx 19.05\%$$

—

Result: About 19.05% of the audience that interacted during the campaign unfollowed.

4. **Net Follower Gain**

Net Gain = New Followers − Unfollows= 3,400 − 800 = 2,600

Result: 2,600 net new followers over 3 months.

5. Engagement per Follower Ratio (Optional)

If average engagement (likes/comments) on posts is known, say 1,260 interactions per post, and the follower count is 12,600, then:

$$\text{Engagement Rate (\%)} = \left(\frac{1,260}{12,600}\right) \times 100 = 10\%$$

Result: 10% engagement rate, a strong signal of content relevance.

Numerical : A beverage company launched a 1-month campaign using the hashtag #MyChillMoment encouraging customers to post pictures with their product.

During the campaign, the following data was collected:

- Total UGC posts using #MyChillMoment: 2,500
- Total likes on UGC posts: 175,000
- Total comments on UGC posts: 25,000
- Brand mentions (outside the hashtag): 1,000
- Average followers per user posting UGC: 800
- Brand's own posts during the campaign: 15 posts
- Engagements on brand's own posts: 36,000
- Conversions attributed to UGC (via tracking links): 1,000 purchases

1. Average Engagement per UGC Post

$$\text{Average Engagement per Post} = \frac{\text{Total Likes + Comments}}{\text{Number of UGC Posts}} = \frac{175,000 + 25,000}{2,500} = \frac{200,000}{2,500} = 80$$

Result: Each UGC post generated an average of **80 engagements.**

2. Estimated Total UGC Reach

Estimated Reach = UGC Posts × Average Followers per User= 2,500×800 = 2,000,000

Result: UGC potentially reached 2 million users organically.

1. UGC Engagement Rate

$$\text{Estimated Reach} = \text{UGC Posts} \times \text{Average Followers per User} = 2,500 \times 800 = 2,000,000$$

Result: The UGC content had a 10% engagement rate, which is considered high.

4. Brand Engagement Comparison (UGC vs. Brand Posts)

Engagement on brand's own posts: 36,000

Engagement on UGC posts: 200,000

UGC Engagement Advantage= 200,000/ 36,000 ≈ 5.56

5. Conversion Rate from UGC

$$\text{Conversion Rate (\%)} = \left(\frac{\text{Conversions from UGC}}{\text{Total UGC Posts}}\right) \times 100 = \left(\frac{1,000}{2,500}\right) \times 100 = 40\%$$

Result: 40% of UGC posts directly contributed to conversions (via link tracking), which is very strong.

1.13 Sociograms in Social Media

A sociogram can be applied to social media networks to visualize relationships, interactions, and influence patterns among users. Platforms like Facebook, Twitter (X), Instagram, and LinkedIn generate vast amounts of connection data that can be mapped to analyze social structures.

They can visually represent:

- Friend/follow relationships (e.g., mutual follows on Twitter)

- Interaction patterns (e.g., likes, comments, retweets, replies)
- Information flow (e.g., how a hashtag or meme spreads)
- Influencers vs. passive users
- Communities or clusters (e.g., political echo chambers)

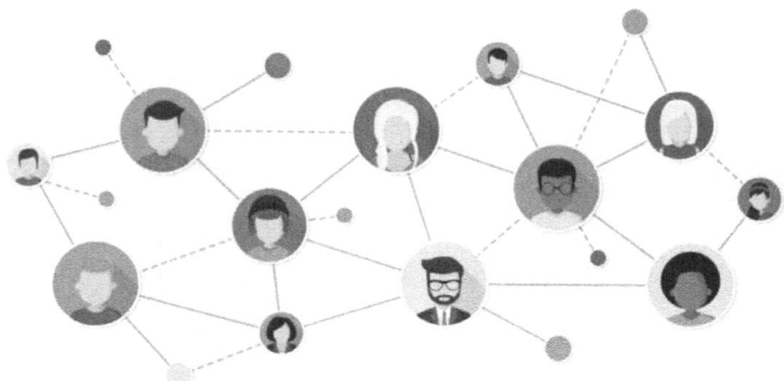

Types of Insights:

Influencer Detection:

- Identify users with the most incoming connections (high in-degree centrality).
- Viral Spread:
- Trace how a post, hashtag, or meme spreads.
- Community Detection:
- Cluster users who interact mostly within subgroups.
- Echo Chambers & Polarization:
- See ideological or topical bubbles in a network.

Tools to Create Social Media Sociograms:

- Gephi (open-source graph visualization tool)
- NodeXL (Excel plugin)
- Netlytic or SocioViz

- Python libraries: NetworkX, igraph, Plotly, Graph-tool
- API data: From platforms like Twitter (via Twitter API)

Real-World Example:

1. Imagine analyzing a hashtag like #ClimateChange on Twitter:
2. Nodes = users tweeting/retweeting
3. Arrows = retweets or replies
4. Larger nodes = high retweet counts
5. Clusters = different ideological camps (activists, skeptics, scientists)

A sociogram here might show:

- ➢ A few influential hubs (celebrities or news orgs)
- ➢ Bridging users who connect different groups
- ➢ Isolated users posting without interaction

1.14 Sociometric studies in Social Media

Sociometry is the scientific measurement of social relationships in groups and was developed by J. L. Moreno by investigating the structure of groups and society.

It involves asking participants to choose whom they prefer to interact with, and mapping those choices into a sociogram.

In social media, instead of asking, we observe behavior:

- Who follows whom
- Who likes/comments/retweets
- Who gets mentioned or tagged

Sociometric Studies in Social Media Examine Table:

Area of Study	What It Analyzes
Popularity	Who gets the most attention or engagement
Reciprocity	Are interactions mutual (e.g., likes exchanged, mutual follows)?
Influence & Leadership	Who shapes opinions, trends, or behaviors?
Group Dynamics	Formation of cliques, clusters, or communities
Exclusion & Isolation	Who is ignored or peripheral to interaction networks?
Sentiment & Trust	Emotional tone or reliability within relationships

Key Aspects of Sociometric Studies in Social Media

1. Data Collection Methods

- Follower/Following Networks (Twitter, Instagram)
- Engagement Metrics (Likes, comments, shares, mentions)
- Content Analysis (Hashtags, keywords, sentiment)
- Surveys & Questionnaires (E.g., asking users about their interactions)

Applications of Sociometric Studies in Social Media

1. Influencer & Community Detection

- Identifies key opinion leaders and micro-influencers.
- Detects echo chambers (groups with similar beliefs).

2. Information & Misinformation Spread

- Tracks how fake news or viral trends propagate.
- Maps bot networks (fake accounts with unusual interaction patterns).

3. Brand & Marketing Analysis

- Measures brand engagement (who talks about a product).
- Finds brand advocates and detractors.

4. Political & Social Research

- Analyzes polarization in political debates.
- Studies social movements (e.g., #MeToo, #BlackLivesMatter).

5. Mental Health & Social Behavior

- Examines loneliness (users with few interactions).
- Detects cyberbullying networks.

Goals of Sociometry

- Facilitate constructive change in individuals and groups.
- Increase awareness, empathy, reciprocity and social interactions.
- Explore social choice patterns and reduce conflicts.
- Clarify roles, interpersonal relations, and values.
- Reveal overt and covert group dynamics.
- Increase group cohesion and productivity.

1.15 Case Study: Twitter Sociometric Analysis

1. Research Question: How does political misinformation spread on Twitter?
2. Collect Data: Gather tweets with a political hashtag (#Election2024).
3. Map Interactions: Identify retweets, mentions, and replies.

Analyze Key Metrics:

- Who are the super-spreaders (high betweenness centrality)?
- Are there bot-like behaviors (low reciprocity, high posting frequency)?

Findings:

- A few verified accounts amplify misinformation.
- Isolated clusters reinforce conspiracy theories.

1.16 Basics of Social Media and Business Models

Social media has revolutionized how businesses interact with customers, market products, and generate revenue. Understanding its core principles and business models is essential for entrepreneurs, marketers, and analysts.

What is Social Media?

Social media refers to digital platforms that enable users to:

- Create & share content (text, images, videos).
- Engage in conversations (likes, comments, shares).
- Build networks (followers, friends, communities).

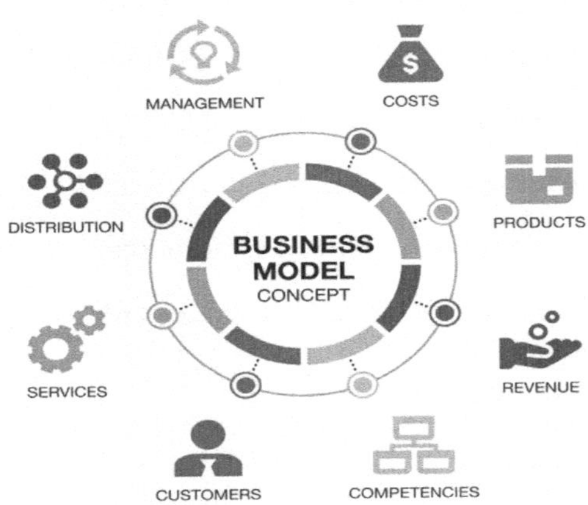

1.17 Social Media Platforms & Their Focus

Platform	Primary Use	Key Features
Facebook	Community-building	Groups, Marketplace, Ads
Instagram	Visual storytelling	Stories, Reels, Influencers
Twitter (X)	Real-time news/discussion	Hashtags, Threads
LinkedIn	Professional networking	B2B marketing, Job postings
TikTok	Short-form video	Viral trends, Algorithm-driven
YouTube	Long-form video	Monetization (Ads, Sponsorships)
Pinterest	Visual discovery	Shopping pins, DIY ideas

Social media platforms primarily offer their services for free to users, but generate revenue through various monetization strategies.

1. Advertising Model (Most common)

- How it works: Platforms sell ad space to businesses. Targeting is based on user data.
- Examples: Facebook Ads, Instagram Sponsored Posts, YouTube Ads
- Tools used: Google Ads, Meta Ads Manager, Twitter Ads

2. Freemium Model

- How it works: Basic features are free, but advanced tools require payment.

- Examples: LinkedIn Premium, YouTube Premium, Snapchat+
- Revenue Source: Monthly subscriptions

3. Influencer/Affiliate Marketing

- How it works: Influencers promote products; platforms may take a cut.
- Indirect Revenue Model but helps platforms grow user engagement.

4. Data Monetization

- How it works: Platforms collect user data (legally) and sell anonymized insights to advertisers and third parties.
- Highly Controversial and under regulatory scrutiny.

5. Marketplace & Commerce

- How it works: Platforms allow users or brands to sell products directly.
- Examples: Facebook Marketplace, Instagram Shopping, TikTok Shop

6. Creator Economy

- How it works: Platforms support content creators through monetization tools.
- Examples: YouTube Partner Program, TikTok Creator Fund, Instagram Subscriptions

7. Virtual Goods and Subscriptions

- How it works: Users pay for virtual gifts, badges, or exclusive content.
- Examples: Twitch subscriptions, TikTok coins, YouTube Super Chat

1.18 Basics of Web Search Engines and Digital Advertising

Search engine advertising (also known as search advertising, Internet search advertising, or online search advertising) allows you to directly display your paid ads among the search results on various search engines, like Google, Bing, and Yahoo.

Components:

- Web Crawling
- Bots (Spiders) scan the web and collect data (e.g., Googlebot).
- Indexing
- Pages are stored in a massive database (Google's index).
- Ranking Algorithms
- Uses 200+ ranking factors (keywords, backlinks, user experience).
- Query Processing
- Understands search intent (e.g., "best laptop" vs. "buy laptop").

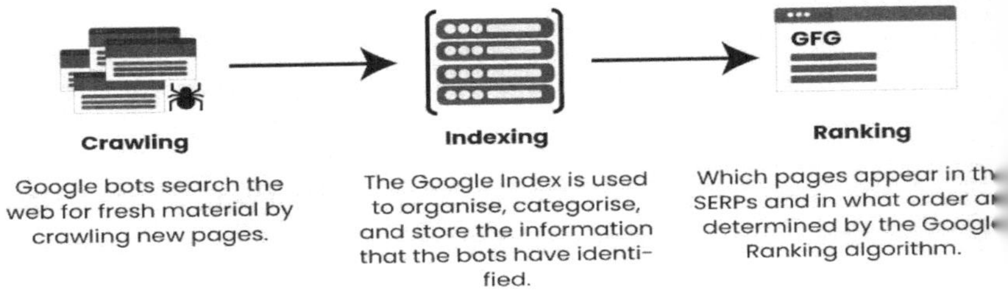

Major Search Engines:

- Google (90%+ market share)
- Bing (Microsoft's engine)
- Yahoo (Powered by Bing)
- DuckDuckGo (Privacy-focused)
- Niche Engines (Ecosia, Yandex, Baidu)

1.19 How Search Engine Marketing Work

Search engine marketing works by the following process:

Step I: There are certain phrases or keywords that consumers use while searching for a product on a website.

Step II: The companies need to list the probable topics in a spreadsheet that they want to rank. The topics listed should correspond with the products and services that they assume will mostly be demanded by the consumer.

Step III: Next they need to broaden the topics and identify the specific keywords or phrases that they think their customers might use or are already using while looking for the product or information. This process of determining the most used keyword is known as keyword analysis. Keyword analysis can be done with the help of certain tools and software such as Google Analytics, WordStream, and Hub Spot's source report. It must be made sure that the keywords are the exact phrases used by the consumers.

Step IV: After bidding for the appropriate keywords, the marketers purchase ad space at the top of search engine result pages so that their advertisements are displayed at a higher rank when searched for the same.

Step V: The payment to the search engine providers is done based on pay-per-click. In this system, every time a user or a consumer clicks on the website's link, it gets tracked and they get their payment based on the number of clicks generated.

1.20 Search Engine Optimization (SEO) vs. Paid Search (SEM)

Aspect	SEO (Organic Search)	SEM (Paid Search)
Cost	Free (but time-consuming)	Pay-per-click (PPC)
Placement	Organic results	Sponsored ads (top/bottom)
Speed	Takes months to rank	Instant visibility

Examples	Blog ranking #1	Google Ads
Aspect	SEO (Organic Search)	SEM (Paid Search)

A. SEO Strategies

- **On-Page SEO (Content,** keywords, meta tags)
- Off-Page SEO (Backlinks, social signals)
- Technical SEO (Site speed, mobile-**friendliness)**

B. SEM Strategies

- **Google Ads (Text,** display, shopping ads)
- Bing Ads (Lower competition, cheaper CPC)
- Retargeting Ads (Follow **users who visited your site)**

1.21 Main Types of Digital Advertising

Type	Description	Example
Search Ads (PPC)	Text ads on search engine results pages.	Google Ads
Display Ads	Banners and images on websites.	Google Display Network
Social Media Ads	Ads on platforms like Facebook, Instagram, Twitter.	Meta Ads, TikTok Ads
Video Ads	Short ads on video platforms.	YouTube pre-roll
Native Ads	Ads that blend with content.	Sponsored posts on news sites
Affiliate Marketing	Promoting products for commission.	Amazon Affiliates
Email Marketing	Promotional messages via email.	Mailchimp, HubSpot

Platforms and Tools

- **Google Ads – search and** display advertising.
- Meta Ads Manager – for Facebook and Instagram.
- Microsoft Ads – for Bing.
- YouTube Ads – video ad placements.
- Ad Networks – e.g., Taboola, Outbrain (for native ads).
- Google Analytics / GA4 – track ad performance and conversions.

1.22 Differences between SEM, SEA and SEO

Aspect	**SEO** (Search Engine Optimization)	**SEA** (Search Engine Advertising)	**SEM** (Search Engine Marketing)
Full Form	Search Engine Optimization	Search Engine Advertising	Search Engine Marketing
Type	**Organic (unpaid)** search optimization	**Paid** search advertising	**Umbrella term** (includes SEO + SEA)
Objective	Improve website's	Display ads in search engine **ad**	Manage both **organic** and **paid**

	organic visibility	slots	search efforts
Cost	No direct cost per click; involves time & effort	**Pay-per-click (PPC)** or impression-based cost	Varies—includes both SEO investment & ad budget
Tools Used	Google Search Console, Ahrefs, SEMrush, Moz	Google Ads, Bing Ads	Both SEO & SEA tools
Time to Results	**Slow** (weeks to months)	**Fast** (immediate after campaign launch)	Mixed: short-term (SEA) + long-term (SEO)
Click-Through Rate (CTR)	Often higher for top organic results	Ads can be skipped or ignored	Combines reach of both
Longevity	Long-lasting with consistent effort	Short-term (only while paying for ads)	Balanced longevity (strategy-dependent)
Examples	Blog optimization, keyword ranking, backlinks	Google Ads text ad appearing at top of results	Combined SEO + Google Ads strategy

Application of SMA in different areas

Area	Application
Marketing & Branding	Track brand sentiment and awareness- Monitor campaign performance- Identify influencers and brand advocates
Customer Service	Detect customer complaints early- Respond to queries in real-time- Improve customer satisfaction
Product Development	Gather feedback from users- Identify trends and feature demands- Analyze competitor product reviews
Sales & Lead Generation	Spot potential leads from social mentions- Use intent-based targeting- Measure

	conversion from social touchpoints
Public Relations	Monitor brand reputation- Detect and manage PR crises- Analyze media coverage and mentions
Human Resources (HR)	Employer branding and sentiment tracking- Recruitment via platforms like LinkedIn- Analyze employee advocacy
Politics & Governance	Track public opinion during elections- Combat misinformation- Analyze engagement on political messages
Healthcare	Track discussions about diseases, vaccines, side effects- Health campaign impact analysis- Monitor misinformation
Education	Understand student feedback- Promote institutional content- Analyze educational trends and engagement
Entertainment & Media	Analyze audience reactions to shows, movies, or events- Trend spotting for content planning- Influence measurement
Retail & eCommerce	Track reviews and product mentions- Optimize influencer campaigns- Measure customer sentiment post-purchase
Finance & Banking	- Gauge customer trust and brand sentiment- Detect early signs of fraud or dissatisfaction- Track discussion of financial trends (e.g., crypto)

Problem: You have 3 web pages: A, B, and C. The link structure is.

- A links to B and C
- B links to C
- C links to A

Calculate PageRank for each page using:

- Damping factor (d) = 0.85
- Initial PageRank = 1 for each page
- Run 1 iteration

Step 1: Page Rank Calculation (1 iteration)

Pages: A, B,

Links:

A → B, C

B → C

C → A

Damping factor, d=0.85

Initial Page Rank, PR(A) = PR(B)= PR(C) =1

Step 1: Understand the formula

$$PR(P_i) = \frac{1-d}{N} + d \times \sum_{P_j \in M(P_i)} \frac{PR(P_j)}{L(P_j)}$$

- N = total pages = 3
- $M(P_i)$ = set of pages linking to P_i
- $L(P_j)$ = number of outbound links from P_j

Step 2: Calculate PRPRPR for each page after 1 iteration

Calculate $PR(A)$:

- Pages linking to A: C (because C → A)
- $L(C) = 1$ (C links only to A)

$$PR(A) = \frac{1-0.85}{3} + 0.85 \times \frac{PR(C)}{L(C)} = 0.05 + 0.85 \times \frac{1}{1} = 0.05 + 0.85 = 0.90$$

Calculate $PR(B)$:

- Pages linking to B: A (because A → B)
- $L(A) = 2$ (A links to B and C)

$$PR(B) = 0.05 + 0.85 \times \frac{PR(A)}{L(A)} = 0.05 + 0.85 \times \frac{1}{2} = 0.05 + 0.425 = 0.475$$

Calculate $PR(C)$:

- Pages linking to C: A and B (A → C, B → C)
- $L(A) = 2, L(B) = 1$

$$PR(C) = 0.05 + 0.85 \times \left(\frac{PR(A)}{L(A)} + \frac{PR(B)}{L(B)}\right) = 0.05 + 0.85 \times \left(\frac{1}{2} + \frac{1}{1}\right) = 0.05 + 0.85 \times 1.5 = 0.05 + 1.275 = 1.325$$

Step 3: Normalize if needed (optional)

Sum of new PR values = 0.90 + 0.475 + 1.325 = 2.7 (should sum to 3, the number of pages)

Normalization factor = 3 / 2.7 = 1.111

Multiply each by 1.111 to normalize:

- $PR(A) = 0.90 \times 1.111 = 1.0$
- $PR(B) = 0.475 \times 1.111 = 0.528$
- $PR(C) = 1.325 \times 1.111 = 1.472$

Problem: A search engine processes **1 million queries/hour**. What is the average query response time if the system handles **50 queries/sec**.

Solution:

$$\text{Queries/sec} = \frac{1,000,000}{3600} \approx 278 \text{ queries/sec}$$

$$\text{Response Time} = \frac{1}{\text{Queries/sec}} = \frac{1}{278} \approx 0.0036 \text{ sec (3.6 ms)}$$

Problem: A website gets **100,000 visitors/month**, with a **2% CTR** and **$0.50 CPC**. What is estimated ad revenue.

$$\text{Clicks} = 100,000 \times 0.02 = 2,000$$

$$\text{Revenue} = 2,000 \times 0.50 = \$1,000$$

Problem: A search engine crawls **10,000 pages/day** but only indexes **7,500**. What is the indexing rate.

$$\text{Indexing Rate} = \left(\frac{\text{Indexed Pages}}{\text{Crawled Pages}}\right) \times 100 = \left(\frac{7500}{10000}\right) \times 100 = 75\%$$

Problem: Two advertisers bid on a keyword:

Advertiser X: Bid = **$2.00**, Quality Score = **8**

Advertiser Y: Bid = **$2.50**, Quality Score = **6**

Which ad ranks higher?

Solution:

Ad Rank = Bid × Quality Score

Advertiser X: 2.00×8=162.00×8=16

Advertiser Y: 2.50×6=152.50×6=15

Problem: A Google Ads campaign spends $300 and generates 200 clicks. What is the CPC (Cost-Per-Click).

$$CPC = \frac{\text{Total Cost}}{\text{Clicks}} = \frac{300}{200} = \$1.50$$

Problem: An ad receives 5,000 impressions and 150 clicks. What is the CTR (Click-Through Rate) ?

$$CTR = \left(\frac{\text{Clicks}}{\text{Impressions}}\right) \times 100 = \left(\frac{150}{5000}\right) \times 100 = 3\%$$

UNIT – II

2.1 Graphs and Matrices in Social Media Analytics

Social media platforms generate vast amounts of interconnected data, making graph theory and matrix algebra essential tools for analyzing relationships, influence, and information flow. Below is an overview of how graphs and matrices are applied in social media analytics.

Representing Social Networks as Graphs

A graph (or network) consists of:

- Nodes (Vertices): Represent users, pages, or entities.
- Edges (Links): Represent relationships (follows, likes, comments, mentions).

Types of Social Media Graphs

- Undirected Graph: Symmetric relationships (e.g., Facebook friendships).
- Directed Graph: Asymmetric relationships (e.g., Twitter follows).
- Weighted Graph: Edges have weights (e.g., engagement strength).
- Bipartite Graph: Connects two types of nodes (e.g., users and posts).

Engagement Matrix

Platform	Likes	Shares	Comments	Engagement Rate
Instagram	2,500	300	600	4.2%
Facebook	1,800	450	550	3.6%
Twitter	1,200	600	300	3.2%

Content Performance Matrix

Post ID	Reach	Engagement	CTR	Conversion
101	5,000	750	1.5%	20
102	8,000	500	0.8%	12

2.2 The adjacency matrix of Social Media Analytics

In Social Media Analytics, an adjacency matrix is a powerful tool to model relationships between users, posts, or entities. It represents a network (graph) where:

- Rows and columns are users or accounts.
- A value of 1 (or another weight) at position (i, j) means that User i interacted with User j.
- A 0 means no interaction.

Basic Adjacency Matrix Example

Let's say we are analyzing a Twitter-like interaction network among 4 users: A, B, C, and D. An interaction can be a mention, retweet, or reply.

	A	**B**	**C**	**D**
A	0	1	1	0
B	0	0	1	1
C	1	0	0	0
D	0	0	1	0

Interpretation:

- A interacted with B and C.
- B interacted with C and D.
- C interacted with A.

- D interacted with C.

From Adjacency Matrix to Graph (Python Example)

```
import pandas as pd

import networkx as nx

import matplotlib.pyplot as plt

# Create adjacency matrix

data = {

    'A': [0, 1, 1, 0],

    'B': [0, 0, 1, 1],

    'C': [1, 0, 0, 0],

    'D': [0, 0, 1, 0]

}

df = pd.DataFrame(data, index=['A', 'B', 'C', 'D'])

# Create graph

G = nx.from_pandas_adjacency(df, create_using=nx.DiGraph())

nx.draw(G, with_labels=True, node_color='lightblue', node_size=2000)

plt.show()
```

2.3 Paths, connectivity in Social Media Analytics

In Social Media Analytics, understanding paths and connectivity in a social graph (network of users) reveals how information spreads, who influences whom, and how tightly-knit communities are. These are fundamental concepts in graph theory applied to social networks.

1. Connectivity in Social Media

- Connectivity refers to whether and how users are linked in a social network. It helps answer questions like:

- Can any user reach another through a series of interactions?
- Are there isolated users or communities?
- How resilient is the network to losing key users (nodes)?

Types of Connectivity

Type	Description	Example in Social Media	Type
Connected Graph	Every user is reachable from every other (in an undirected network).	All users in a group chat.	Connected Graph
Strongly Connected	In a directed graph, every node is reachable from every other both ways.	Mutual interactions on Twitter or LinkedIn.	Strongly Connected
Weakly Connected	Nodes are reachable if directions are ignored.	You may follow someone, but they don't follow back.	Weakly Connected
Weakly Connected	Nodes are reachable if directions are ignored.	You may follow someone, but they don't follow back.	Weakly Connected

2. Paths in Social Media

A path is a sequence of users where each user interacts with the next. Studying paths helps track:

- Information diffusion (how a tweet or video spreads)
- Viral trends
- Influencer reach
- Shortest/quickest communication chains

Path Types

Path Type	Description	Example
Simple Path	No user is repeated	A → B → C
Cycle	Starts and ends at the same user	A → B → C → A
Shortest Path	Fewest interactions between two users	Influencer to follower in 2 steps

Connectivity Metrics in Practice

Metric	Meaning	Tool
Degree Centrality	Number of direct connections (followers, mentions)	NetworkX, Gephi
Closeness Centrality	How close a user is to all others (lower = more central)	Detects fast spreaders
Betweenness Centrality	How often a user is on the shortest path between others	Finds gatekeepers or bridges
Connected Components	Disconnected user groups (e.g., multiple unconnected subgroups)	Finds isolated or niche communities

2.4 Distance and Breadth First Search in Social Media Analytics

Distance metrics and BFS are fundamental tools for analyzing social networks, enabling applications from influencer detection to content spread prediction.

Distance in Social Media Graphs

Distance is the shortest path length (number of edges/interactions) between two users or entities in the social network.

Use Cases of Distance:

Use Case	Description
Influencer Reach	How close an influencer is to average users (smaller = more reachable).
Virality Measurement	How far a post traveled in terms of user-to-user chains.
Recommendation Systems	Users with smaller social distance might have similar interests.

Example:

If User A reposts a video and then User B shares it, then C, and then D:

Distance(A, D) = 3

Breadth-First Search (BFS) in Social Media

- Breadth-First Search is an algorithm to traverse or search a graph level by level. It's ideal for:
- Finding shortest paths in un weighted graphs
- Discovering followers or interaction layers
- Detecting influencer reach in levels

BFS Process:

- Start from a node (e.g. user A)
- Visit all direct connections (1st degree)

- Then visit their connections (2nd degree), and so on

Q. Suppose we have the following **directed social interaction graph**:

A → B → D

A → C → E

C → F

Edges:

(A, B), (A, C), (B, D), (C, E), (C, F)

We want to perform **BFS starting from node A**.

Adjacency List Representation

A: [B, C]

B: [D]

C: [E, F]

D: [ ]

E: [ ]

F: [ ]

Breadth-First Search from Node A

- We'll explore level by level, tracking:
- Visited nodes
- Queue
- Levels (distance from A)

Initialization:

- Visited: {A}
- Queue: [A]
- Level: A → 0

Step-by-Step BFS Traversal

Step	Current Node	Queue	Visited	Level
1	A	[B, C]	{A, B, C}	B: 1, C: 1
2	B	[C, D]	{A, B, C, D}	D: 2
3	C	[D, E, F]	{A, B, C, D, E, F}	E: 2, F: 2
4	D	[E, F]	—	—
5	E	[F]	—	—
6	F	[]	—	—

Final BFS Output (Levels from A)

Node	Distance (Level from A)
A	0
B	1
C	1
D	2
E	2
F	2

Interpretation in Social Media Analytics

- A = Influencer
- Level 1 (B, C): Directly engaged users
- Level 2 (D, E, F): Indirectly reached users (e.g., via retweet or share)

2.5 Network Datasets in Social Media numerical solution

real-world social network datasets, their numerical representations, and computational methods for analysis using Python.

- Common Social Network Datasets
- Numerical Representations (Matrices)
- Key Algorithms with Python Implementations
- Practical Application

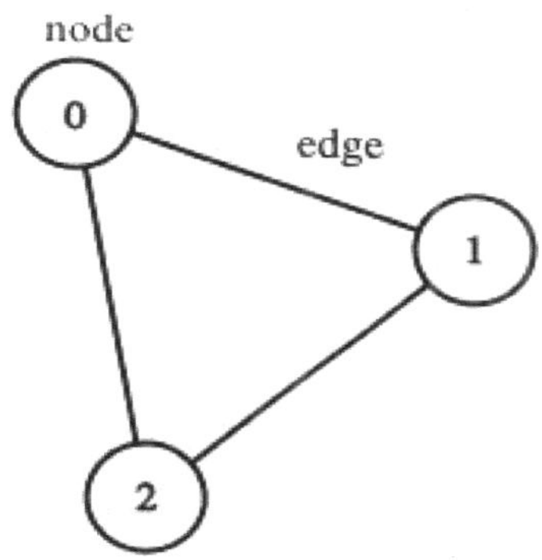

1. Popular Social Network Datasets

Dataset	Nodes	Edges	Description	Source
Facebook Social Circles	4,039	88,234	Friend connections	SNAP
Twitter Follow Graphs	81,306	1,768,149	Who-follows-whom	Konect
Reddit Hyperlinks	55,863	858,490	Subreddit connections	SNAP
YouTube Social Network	1,134,890	2,987,624	User interactions	SNAP

Dataset Characteristics

Format: Typically edge lists (user1, user2) or adjacency matrices

Types:

Undirected (Facebook friendships)

Directed (Twitter follows)

Weighted (Number of interactions)

Temporal (Time-stamped interactions)

Numerical Representations

Adjacency Matrix (A)

For a network with N nodes:

Aij=1if edge exists between node *i* and *j*

Aij=0 otherwise

Nodes & ties

Term	**Definition**
Node	A user, account, or entity in a social media network.
Tie (or edge)	A connection or interaction between two nodes (e.g., a follow, retweet, mention).
Directed Tie	A → B means A interacted with B (direction matters).
Weighted Tie	A → B (3) means A interacted with B **3 times**.

Example Dataset: Nodes & Ties

We define a small directed and weighted graph with 5 users (nodes): A, B, C, D, E

Interactions (Ties)

From	To	Weight (Interaction Count)
A	B	2
A	C	1
B	D	3
C	D	1
D	E	1
E	A	1

Numerical Representation: Adjacency Matrix

	A	B	C	D	E
A	0	2	1	0	0
B	0	0	0	3	0
C	0	0	0	1	0
D	0	0	0	0	1
E	1	0	0	0	0

Number of Nodes and Ties

Number of Nodes: **5 (A, B, C, D, E)**

Number of Ties (edges): **6 (from the table above)**

In-Degree and Out-Degree (Numerical)

Node	Out-Degree	In-Degree
A	2	1 (from E)
B	1	1 (from A)
C	1	1 (from A)

D	1	2 (from B, C)
E	1	1 (from D)

Tie Strength (Weight Sum)

Node	Outgoing Weight	Incoming Weight
A	3 (2+1)	1 (from E)
B	3	2 (from A)
C	1	1 (from A)
D	1	4 (from B, C)
E	1	1 (from D)

Influencers

An influencer is a node (user) in a social graph who has:

- High centrality (many or important connections)
- High reach (short distances to others)
- High tie strength (frequent interactions)

Example Dataset: User Interaction Network

Let's consider 6 users: A, B, C, D, E, F
Directed edges = interactions (e.g., mentions, retweets)

Interactions Table

From	To	Interactions (Weight)
A	B	2
A	C	3
B	D	4
C	D	2
D	E	1

F	A	2
E	B	1

Graph Metrics to Identify Influencers

In-Degree Centrality

Number of times a user is interacted with (count of incoming edges).

Node	In-Degree
A	1 (from F)
B	2 (A, E)
C	1 (A)
D	2 (B, C)
E	1 (D)
F	0

Influencer: **B, D** (most targeted by others)

Weighted In-Degree

Sum of interaction weights received by a user.

Node	Weighted In-Degree
A	2 (from F)
B	3 (A=2, E=1)
C	3 (from A)
D	6 (B=4, C=2)
E	1 (from D)
F	0

Influencer: **D (6)** → Highest engagement received

Betweenness Centrality

Measures how often a node lies on the shortest path between other nodes (acts as a bridge).

Manual Estimation (simplified):

A connects F → B/C → D → E

D is a common path to reach E

A and D likely have high betweenness

D and **A** are structural bridges (important intermediaries).

Final Ranking: Influencer Scores

User	In-Degree	Weighted In-Degree	Role
D	2	**6**	High engagement receiver
B	**2**	3	Frequently tagged
A	1	2	Source and bridge
C	1	3	Intermediate connector
E	1	1	Passive receiver
F	0	0	No influence

Conclusion: Top Influencers

D – Most interactions received and central in the graph

B – Frequently targeted by others

A – Key bridge from source (F) to others

2.6 Making connections

Making connections" refers to identifying, measuring, and analyzing the relationships (ties) between users, brands, or content. These connections help you understand influence, spread, community dynamics, and engagement potential.

Types of Connections in Social Media

Connection Type	Description	Example
Follows	One user follows another	A follows B
Mentions	One user tags another in a post	A mentions B in a tweet
Replies/Comments	One user responds to another	B replies to A's post
Shares/Retweets	Content is passed from one user to another	A retweets C
Likes/Reactions	Engagement with content	A likes B’s post

Numerical Example: User Connections Graph

Let’s use 5 users: A, B, C, D, E

Each interaction (connection) is weighted by frequency (number of times one user interacted with another).

Interactions Table

From	To	Interaction Type	Weight (Count)
A	B	Mention	3
A	C	Comment	2
B	D	Retweet	1
C	D	Mention	2
D	E	Follow	1
E	A	Comment	1

Adjacency Matrix (Weighted)

	A	B	C	D	E
A	0	3	2	0	0
B	0	0	0	1	0
C	0	0	0	2	0
D	0	0	0	0	1
E	1	0	0	0	0

Connection Metrics

Out-Degree (Users Actively Connecting)

User	Out-Degree
A	2
B	1
C	1
D	1
E	1

A is making the most connections — a potential initiator or influencer.

In-Degree (Users Being Connected To)

User	In-Degree
A	1 (from E)
B	1 (from A)
C	1 (from A)
D	2 (from B, C)
E	1 (from D)

D is the most connected receiver — content hub or popular user.

Types of Social Connection Analysis

Analysis Type	Goal
• Reachability	Who can reach whom through connections?
• Reciprocity	Are interactions mutual (A ↔ B)?
• Clustering	Are users forming tightly-knit groups?
• Path Length	How many steps does it take to connect two users?
• Tie Strength	How strong or frequent is the connection?

Insights from "Making Connections"

Insight	Example
Identify Influencers	A initiates many ties; D is a central receiver
Viral Spread Paths	A → C → D → E shows how content might flow
Engagement Strategy	Focus on A and D for initial and extended reach
Community Detection	If B and C both point to D, D may be a group hub

Summary

Metric	Value
Total Users (Nodes)	5
Total Connections	6
Strongest Connector	A (outgoing)
Central Target	D (incoming)
Longest Chain	A → C → D → E

2.7 Random graphs and network evolution

A random graph is a network where nodes and edges are added randomly based on probability. It's a useful mathematical model for simulating real social media networks where connections aren't deterministic.

Common Random Graph Models

2.8 Erdős–Rényi (ER)

The Erdős–Rényi (ER) model is one of the simplest and most fundamental models used to represent randomly connected networks — including early-stage or unstructured social media networks.

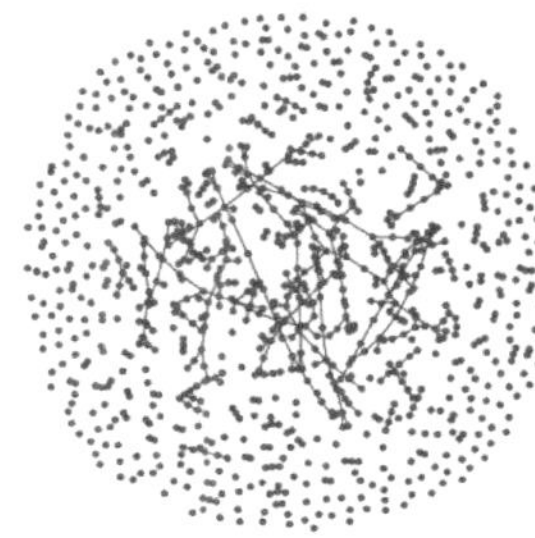

There are two main ER models:

1. **G(n, p)**

n = number of nodes (users)

p = probability that each pair of nodes is connected

Each possible edge is included independently with probability p

2. **G(n, m)**

n = number of nodes

m = fixed number of edges randomly chosen

For social media analytics, we typically use **G(n, p)**

Q.Numerical Example: ER G(n, p)

Let's generate an ER random graph with:

n = 5 users: A, B, C, D, E

p = 0.4 (40% chance of connection between each pair)

Step 1: Total Possible Edges

For an **undirected** graph:

$$\text{Total possible edges} = \frac{n(n-1)}{2} = \frac{5 \times 4}{2} = 10$$

List of all possible edges:

- (A–B), (A–C), (A–D), (A–E)
- (B–C), (B–D), (B–E)

- (C–D), (C–E)
- (D–E)

Step 2: Apply Probability p = 0.4

We simulate each edge randomly — roll a dice (or use random numbers). Let's say we get:

Edge	Add? (Yes if < 0.4)
A–B	☑
A–C	✖
A–D	☑
A–E	✖
B–C	☑
B–D	✖
B–E	☑
C–D	✖
C–E	✖
D–E	☑

Final ER Network:

Edges: A–B, A–D, B–C, B–E, D–E
Graph is sparse and random — no patterns or clusters.

Key Metrics from ER Graph

Metric	Value
Nodes	5
Edges	5 (random)

Avg Degree	$2 \times 5/5=2$
Clustering	Very low
Community Structure	None

2.9 Barabási–Albert (BA) model

The Barabási–Albert (BA) model simulates how real social networks grow, especially those that include influencers or viral hubs.

This model is widely used in social media analytics to understand:

- The emergence of influencers
- Scale-free networks
- Power-law degree distributions

Mechanisms

- Growth: Network expands by adding new nodes over time
- Preferential Attachment: New nodes connect to existing nodes with probability proportional to their degree

2.10 Watts–Strogatz (WS) model

Watts-Strogatz model explains how **small-world networks** emerge in social media, combining high clustering with short path lengths - characteristics observed in Facebook friendships, professional networks, and community structures.

The WS model combines:

- High clustering (tight-knit friend groups)
- Short average path lengths (you can reach anyone in a few steps)

This mimics real social media, where:

- Friends of friends often know each other (clustering)

- Any two users are separated by only a few intermediaries (small-world)

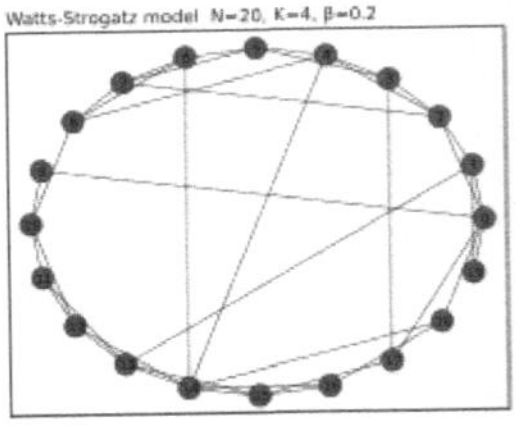

How the WS Model Works

Input Parameters:

1. n: Number of nodes (users)
2. k: Each node is connected to k nearest neighbors in a ring (even number)
3. p: Probability of rewiring each edge ($0 \leq p \leq 1$)

Steps:

1. Start with a regular ring lattice (each node connected to k neighbors).
2. For each edge, with probability p, rewire it to another random node.

2.11 Hypergraphs in social media analytics

Traditional graphs model pairwise relationships (user A connects to user B). But social media often involves group interactions — group chats, shared posts, hashtags, or communities — where multiple users interact simultaneously.

Hypergraphs model these multi-way interactions more naturally and powerfull.

What is a Hypergraph?

A hypergraph is a generalization of a graph:

Nodes (vertices) represent users, posts, or entities.

Hyperedges can connect two or more nodes simultaneously.

Hyperedge: Connects any number of nodes (unlike edges in simple graphs)

Incidence Matrix: Represents node-hyperedge relationships

k-Uniform Hypergraph: All hyperedges have cardinality k (e.g., 3-uniform = all triangles)

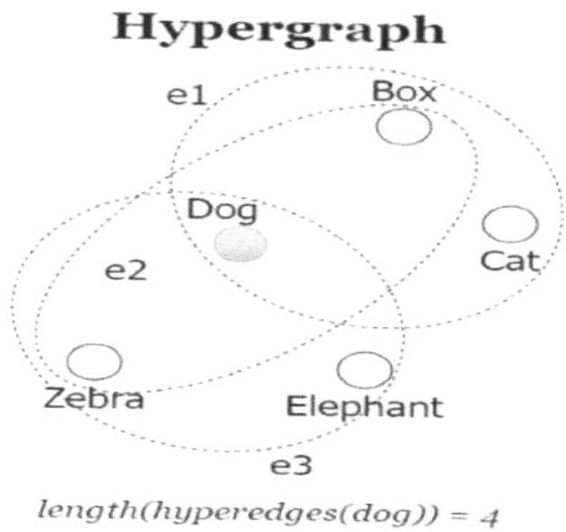

2.12 Social Media Scenarios Where Hyper graphs Shine

Scenario	Why Use a Hypergraph
Hashtag usage	A post using #AI, #Tech, #GPT links all users/posts to the same hyperedge
Group chats / forums	One message connects all participants
Photo tags	One image tagged with multiple users = 1 hyperedge
Collaborative content	Multiple creators linked through a shared project/video
Retweet groups	Many users retweeting the same tweet = joint interaction

2.13 Hypergraph vs Traditional Graph

Feature / Aspect	Traditional Graph	Hypergraph
Connection Type	Pairwise (A–B)	Group-wise (A–B–C–D in one edge)
Edge Definition	Connects **two nodes**	Connects **two or more**

	only	**nodes** simultaneously
Data Structure	Edge list or adjacency matrix	Incidence matrix or set-based hyperedges
Group Interactions	Requires multiple pairwise links	Naturally modeled as one hyperedge
Social Media Use Case	Likes, follows, DMs	Hashtags, group chats, co-tagging, shared posts
Clustering & Communities	Detected via triangles or paths	Inherent in hyperedges (co-participation)
Realism for Social Media	Moderate	**High** (captures multi-user behavior)
Influence Modeling	Based on degree or centrality	Based on hyperedge participation & cardinality
Example Scenario	A retweets B	A, B, C share or comment on the same post
Visualization Complexity	Simple	More complex (often needs bipartite or projection)
Implementation	Easy (many libraries)	Harder (fewer tools, higher complexity)
Libraries/Tools	NetworkX, iGraph	HyperNetX, PyHypergraph, Hypergraphs.

UNIT –III

3.1 Network Structures

The network structure of social media refers to the way users (people or entities) are connected to each other through various platforms (like Facebook, Twitter/X, Instagram, LinkedIn, etc.). These structures determine how information flows, how influence spreads, and how communities form online.

Basic Components of a Social Media Network

Nodes (Vertices)- Individuals, users, pages, groups, or any entities that participate in the network.

Edges (Links)-The connections between users — like friendships, follows, likes, comments, tags, or shares. These can be directed (A follows B) or undirected (A and B are friends).

3.2 Types of Network Structures in Social Media

a. Ego Networks

In social media, an ego network, or egocentric network, focuses on the social connections of a single individual (the "ego") and their direct connections (the "alters"). It's a way to analyze social networks by examining how one person's relationships are structured and how those relationships impact them.

Ego: The individual at the center of the network.

Alter: A person directly connected to the ego.

Ties: The relationships between the ego and alters, and between alters themselves.

How it works:

1. Focus on a Single Individual:

Instead of analyzing the entire social network, ego network analysis zooms in on one person's social connections.

2. Mapping Connections:

It maps out who the ego is connected to (their alters) and the relationships between those alters.

3. Analyzing Network Structure:

It examines the characteristics of the ego network, such as the size, density, and composition of the network, to understand how the ego's social ties influence them.

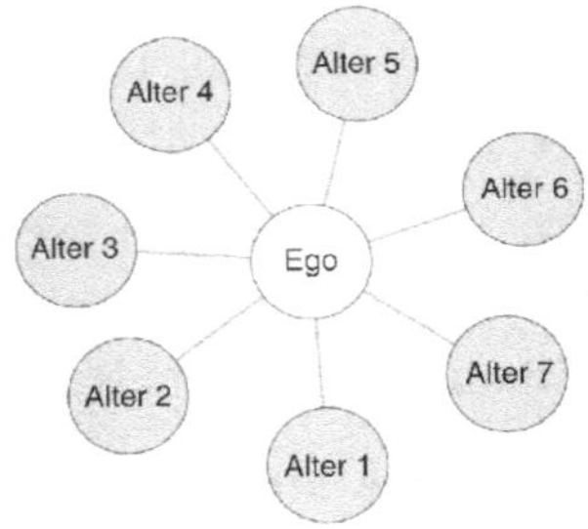

Example:

Imagine a user on Facebook. Their ego network would consist of their friends (alters) and the connections between those friends. The analysis might explore how the user's friends influence their opinions, information they receive, or their social behavior.

Applications:

Understanding Information Diffusion: How information spreads through different parts of the network.

Studying Social Influence: How the opinions and behaviors of alters affect the ego.

Analyzing Social Support: How the ego's network provides emotional support.

Recommender Systems: Understanding how link recommendations can impact the growth and diversity of ego networks.

Public Health: Analyzing how social connections influence health behaviors and outcomes.

- Centered around one user.
- Shows that user's direct connections.
- Example: Your friend circle on Facebook or followers on Instagram.

b. Global (Whole) Network

A global social media network refers to the interconnected web of users and platforms that span across the entire world, facilitating communication and information sharing on a massive scale. Social media platforms with global reach, like Facebook, Instagram, and TikTok, enable users to connect with individuals and communities regardless of geographical boundaries. This global connectivity has profound implications for various aspects of society, including communication, culture, and business.

c. Community Structures

Community structures in social media refer to groups of users who are more connected to each other than to the rest of the network, often formed around shared interests, demographics, or affiliations. These structures are important for understanding user behavior, influence, and information flow within social media platforms.

Aspects of Community Structures:

Formation:

Communities emerge from users' interactions, forming clusters based on shared interests, demographics (age, location, etc.), or social connections.

Dense Connections:

Within a community, users tend to have more connections and interactions with each other than with users outside the community.

Overlapping Communities:

Individuals can belong to multiple communities, creating overlapping structures.

Community Detection:

Identifying these structures is a core task in social network analysis, often achieved through algorithms that analyze user connections and interactions.

Examples of Communities:

Interest-based: Groups focused on specific hobbies, sports, or academic fields.

Demographic: Communities based on age, location, or profession.

Social: Groups formed around friendships, family ties, or professional relationships.

Directed vs. Undirected Networks

In social media, directed networks represent one-way relationships (like following on Twitter), while undirected networks represent reciprocal relationships (like friendships on Facebook). A directed network has connections with a specific direction, while an undirected network's connections are bidirectional.

Directed Networks:

Definition: In a directed network, the connection between two nodes (users) has a specific direction, indicating a one-way relationship.

Example: On Twitter, if user A follows user B, this is a directed edge from A to B. It doesn't necessarily mean that user B also follows user A.

Undirected Networks:

Definition: In an undirected network, connections between nodes are reciprocal. If node A is connected to node B, it implies a connection from B to A as well.

Example:

On Facebook, if user A is friends with user B, this is a mutual, undirected connection. They are both considered friends with each other.

Representation: Undirected networks are usually visualized with simple lines or edges, without arrows, to indicate the bidirectional nature of the relationship.

Equivalence in Social Media:

In social media network analysis, the concept of equivalence helps us understand when two or more users (or nodes) play similar roles or have similar positions in the network — even if they are not directly connected.

There are three main types of equivalence used in analyzing social media networks:

1.Structural Equivalence

2. Automorphic Equivalence

3. Regular Equivalence

3.3 Structural Equivalence

In social media analytics, structural equivalence refers to nodes (users) in a network having identical connections to other nodes. This means they are connected to the same set of individuals, implying similar roles and positions within the network. While perfect structural equivalence is rare, it can be approximated to identify groups with similar influence or behaviors.

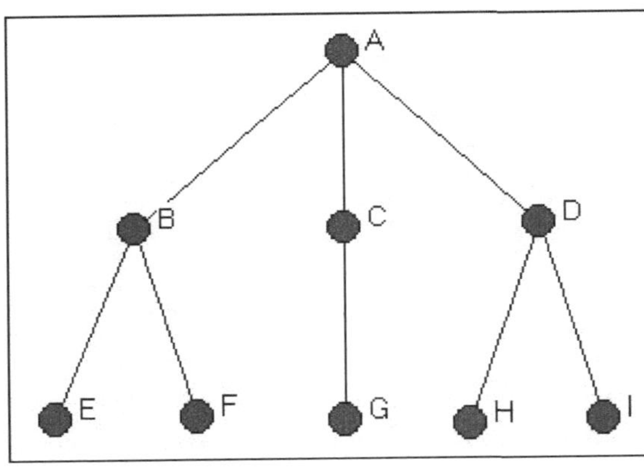

Two users (say, User A and User B) are structurally equivalent if:

They are connected to exactly the same users, in exactly the same way.

This is a strict and rare form of equivalence in social networks, but it's useful for uncovering hidden insights.

Example in Social Media:

Imagine a Twitter scenario:

User	Follows
A	**X, Y, Z**

| B | X, Y, Z |

Here, Users A and B are structurally equivalent — they follow the exact same people, and if they are followed by the same users too, that reinforces the equivalence.

3.4 Automorphic Equivalence

Automorphic Equivalence is a concept from social network analysis used to identify users who occupy similar positions in the network structure — even if they are not directly connected to the same people. In social media analytics, automorphic equivalence helps detect role similarity, community symmetry, or structural redundancy, which is especially useful for group analysis, bot networks, and hierarchical role detection.

Let's say a company runs two regional Facebook pages, each with:

- One admin
- A similar number of followers
- A similar structure (posts, likes, engagement types)

Even if followers differ, their positions are automorphically equivalent because the structure of their roles in the network is symmetric.

Real-World Social Media Applications

- Reddit: Identifying similar moderation structures across subreddits.
- Instagram: Spotting influencer networks with mirrored follower structures.
- X (Twitter): Detecting sock puppet or bot accounts with repetitive connection graphs.
- Discord or Telegram: Mapping similar admin-member relationship hierarchies.

Regular Equivalence

In social network analysis, regular equivalence identifies actors who have similar relationships with other actors in the network, effectively defining social roles based on connection patterns rather than just individual attributes. This concept is valuable for understanding how different users or accounts behave on social media by grouping them into roles based on their network interactions.

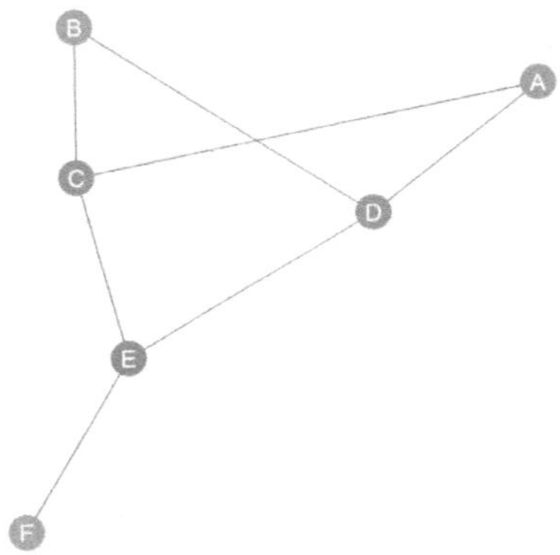

Example in Social Media:

In a Twitter network, all influencers may not follow the exact same people but tend to be followed by many regular users and may also follow similar types of accounts (like news sources).

Similarly, content creators may regularly interact with their audiences but not necessarily the same audience members.

3.5 Homophile

In social media analytics, homophily refers to the tendency for users to connect with and interact with others who are similar to them. This can manifest in various ways, including shared interests, demographics, or opinions. Understanding homophily is crucial for social media analysis as it impacts information diffusion, community formation, and the overall dynamics of online social networks.

Aspects of homophily in social media analysis:

Formation of online communities:

Homophily can lead to the formation of distinct online communities where users with similar characteristics and viewpoints interact primarily with each other.

Information diffusion:

Similar individuals tend to share information and opinions within their groups. This can lead to the rapid spread of information within a community but also create echo chambers where diverse perspectives are limited.

Impact on social influence:

Homophily can influence how users are affected by social influence. Users are more likely to adopt behaviors, opinions, or trends prevalent within their homophilous groups.

Examples of homophily in social media:

Age and location: Users may connect with others of similar age groups or who live in the same geographic location.

Interests and hobbies: Individuals interested in specific sports, music genres, or hobbies may form online communities around these shared interests.

Political or ideological alignment: Users with similar political or ideological viewpoints may connect with each other and form echo chambers on social media platforms.

Language and cultural background: People may connect with others who speak the same language or share a similar cultural background.

3.6 Clustering in Social Media Analytics

Clustering in social media analytics refers to the process of grouping users, posts, or content into clusters based on similarity or connection patterns. These clusters help analysts uncover communities, behavioral patterns, influence zones, and content trends within a social network.

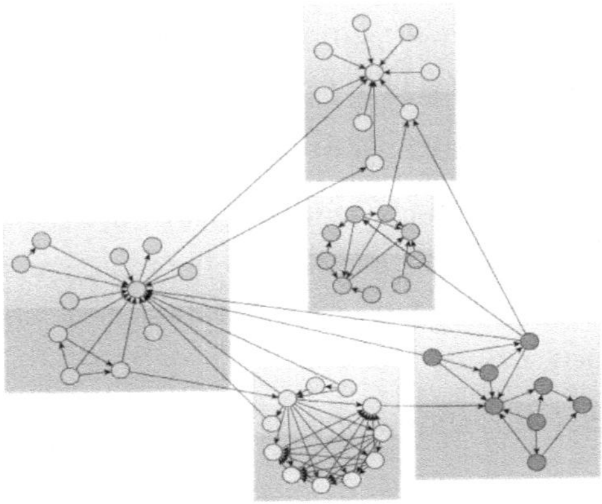

Types of Clustering in Social Media:

1. User Clustering

- Group users based on:
- Follower/following patterns
- Shared likes, comments, hashtags
- Geographic or demographic similarities

2. Content Clustering

- Group posts or messages by:
- Topics or keywords (using NLP or topic modeling)
- Sentiment (positive, negative, neutral)
- Media types (image, video, text)

3. Network Clustering / Community Detection

- Use graph theory to cluster nodes (users) in a network graph based on their connections (edges). Techniques include:
- Modularity-based methods (e.g., Louvain algorithm)

- Label Propagation
- Spectral Clustering

Clustering Techniques & Tools:

Algorithms:

- K-Means (for numeric or feature data like post metrics)
- DBSCAN (for density-based clustering)
- Hierarchical Clustering
- Louvain Method (for network-based community detection)

Tools/Libraries:

- Python: scikit-learn, networkx, igraph, community, nltk, gensim
- Gephi: For interactive network clustering visualization
- Pajek, UCINET, R igraph: For social network research

Real-World Examples:

- Twitter: Cluster users into communities based on retweets, hashtags, or mentions (e.g., political groups, fandoms).
- Instagram: Cluster influencers and followers by content types or interaction patterns.
- Facebook: Detect friendship circles or interest-based groups via mutual friend networks.
- Reddit: Cluster subreddits based on shared users or post topics.

3.7 Snowball sampling

Snowball sampling is a non-probability sampling technique where existing study participants help recruit future subjects from among their acquaintances. It's often used when the target population is hard to reach or when studying sensitive topics, as it leverages social networks for recruitment. The sample grows like a "snowball" as more participants are referred by initial subjects.

Acceptable alternatives that reach the same potential subjects include:

- The study team member may provide information to subjects and encourage them to pass it on to others who may be interested or eligible. The information provided to enrolled subjects (fliers, letters of explanation, etc.) must be approved by the IRB. Interested prospective participants could then contact the project for more info and possible inclusion.
- The study team member may ask subjects to obtain permission from others prior to disclosing their contact information. In this scenario, the researcher would not directly contact the referred/potential subject without permission from the potential subject and would not have access to any information about a potential subject without permission from that individual.

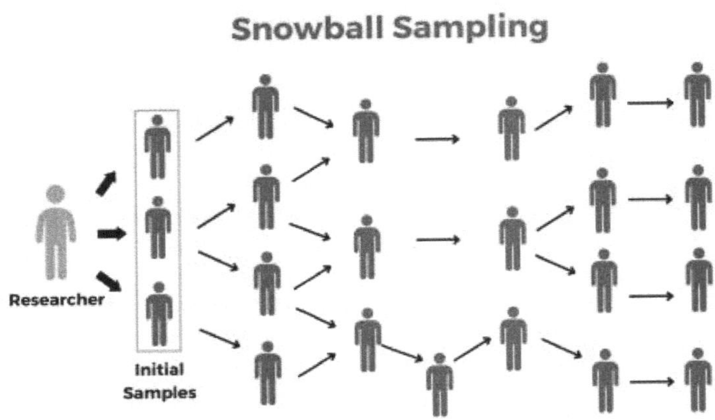

It's especially useful when studying hidden, hard-to-reach, or niche populations, such as:

- Drug users
- Underground communities
- Political activists

- Specialized social media groups

How It Works:

- Start with a seed group (a few initial participants).
- Ask them to refer others they know who meet the criteria.
- Referred participants are then asked to refer more people.
- This continues until the desired sample size or saturation is reached.

Example (in Social Media Context):

- Let's say you're studying a niche group of cryptocurrency influencers on Twitter:
- You start with 3 known crypto influencers.
- Each one gives you the usernames of others they interact with frequently.
- You contact or analyze those new users.
- They then lead you to more crypto influencers.
- A network of connected influencers forms, revealing the structure and key players.

Applications in Social Media Analytics:

Use Case	Description
Influencer Discovery	Identify and expand networks of niche or micro-influencers.
Community Mapping	Find hidden sub-communities by following interaction trails.
Botnet Analysis	Track fake or bot accounts spreading misinformation.
Viral Campaign Tracking	Follow the chain of users sharing a viral post or hashtag.

Types of Snowball Sampling:

Type	Description
• Linear Snowball	Each participant refers only one new participant.
• Exponential Snowball	Each participant refers multiple new participants.
• Exponential Non-discriminative	Every referred individual becomes a recruiter.
• Exponential Discriminative	Only selected referrals become recruiters.

3.8 Contact tracing and random walks

Contact Tracing and Random Walks are two analytical methods used in network science, epidemiology, and increasingly in social media analytics, to understand how information, influence, or even viruses (literal or digital) spread through a network.

Contact Tracing in Networks

Contact tracing refers to the process of identifying and following the paths of contact between individuals in a network — commonly used in public health but applicable in digital networks too.

In Epidemiology:

- If Person A tests positive for an infectious disease, contact tracing identifies everyone they were in close contact with over a given period.
- It maps out who-infected-whom or who-interacted-with-whom.

In Social Media Analytics:

Can be used to trace the origin and spread of:

- Viral posts or hashtags
- Misinformation or rumors

- Bots spreading spam
- Digital content adoption (memes, challenges, etc.)

Example:

If a fake news article goes viral on Facebook:

- Contact tracing helps identify who first posted it, who shared it next, and how it propagated through the network.
- You get a tree-like diffusion structure of influence.

Random Walks in Networks

A random walk is a process where a "walker" (or signal) moves randomly from one node to a connected node, and continues doing this over time.

Used for:

- PageRank algorithm (used by Google to rank websites)
- Community detection in large networks
- Similarity measures in recommendation engines
- Sampling large graphs when full traversal is expensive

In Social Media:

A random walk could simulate how a user discovers new content or connections, e.g., by liking a post, following a related user, seeing recommended content, and so on.

Used to:

- Rank influential users
- Estimate network centrality
- Find short paths or influential chains

Tools & Libraries:

- NetworkX (Python): Can simulate both contact tracing and random walks.

- igraph / SNAP / Gephi: Good for visualizing propagation and stochastic movement.

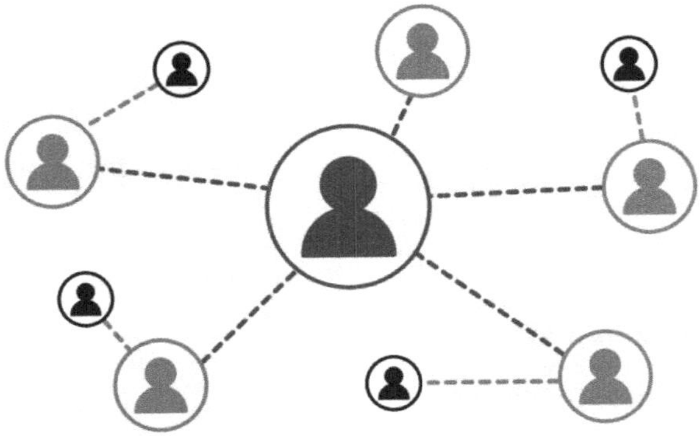

Applications to Contact Tracing:

Modeling disease spread: A random walk on a contact network simulates how an infected person might transmit the disease.

Prioritizing contacts: Not all contacts are equal—some individuals (super-spreaders) contribute more to transmission. Random walks help identify high-risk paths.

Optimizing testing/tracing: Instead of testing everyone, random walk-based sampling can efficiently find clusters (e.g., "friendship paradox"—a person's contacts are, on average, more connected than themselves).

3.9 Ego-centric networks

Ego-centric networks (or shortened to "ego" networks) are a particular type of network which specifically maps the connections of and from the perspective of a single person (an "ego"). For example, if you were to ask someone to name their friends (or any other type of "alter," which is defined as someone who is not the ego), they will tell you who their friends are. However, they will not tell you who the friends of other people are.

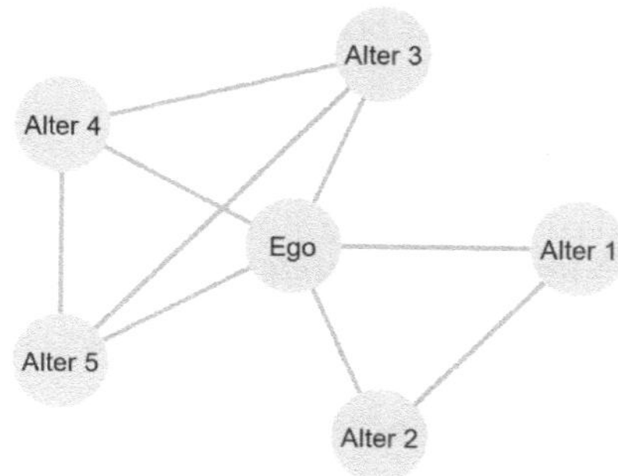

- **Ego**: The focal person in the network (e.g., a COVID-positive patient).
- **Alters**: People directly connected to the ego (e.g., those the ego has been in contact with).
- **Ties**: Relationships or interactions between ego and alters, and possibly among alters themselves.

Example Problem: Contact Tracing with Ego-Centered Network

Problem Statement: A person (Ego) has had close contact with 5 people (Alters A, B, C, D, and E) during a week. The number of contacts (interactions) per alter is:

Alter	No. of Contacts
A	3
B	5
C	2
D	4
E	6

Each contact has a 10% probability of transmitting the disease.

Questions:

- What is the total number of contacts?

- What is the probability that at least one alter gets infected?
- Which alter is most at risk?

Solution

1. Total Number of Contacts

Just sum up the contacts: 3+5+2+4+6=20 contacts

2. Probability that at least one alter gets infected

Let's assume infection risk per contact is independent and 10%, so the probability that a contact does not result in infection is 90% or 0.9.

We calculate the probability that no alter gets infected, then subtract from 1.

P(no infection)=$0.9^{20} \approx$ 0.1216

P(at least one infection)=$1-0.9^{20} \approx 1-0.1216 = 0.8784$

So, there is an 87.84% chance that at least one person is infected.

3. Which alter is most at risk?

We calculate the probability that each alter does **not** get infected:

Alter A: $0.9^3=0.729 \Rightarrow$ Risk=$1-0.729 = 0.271$

Alter B: $0.9^5=0.590 \Rightarrow$ Risk=$1-0.590 = 0.410$

Alter C: $0.9^2=0.81 \Rightarrow$ Risk=$1-0.81= 0.190$

Alter D: $0.9^4=0.656 \Rightarrow$ Risk=$1-0.656 = 0.344$

Alter E: $0.9^6=0.531 \Rightarrow$ Risk=$1-0.531=0.469$

Alter E is most at risk with a 46.9% chance of infection.

3.10 Dominance hierarchies

Dominance hierarchies are a concept from social behavior studies—used in animal behavior, sociology, and even epidemiology and contact tracing—to model structured relationships of power, status, or influence within a group.

They're especially useful when:

- Modeling **who influences whom** in spreading behavior or infection
- Assessing **priority of testing or intervention** in outbreaks (e.g., who has most contacts or control)

Concepts of Dominance Hierarchies

- **Dominance**: The ability of an individual (or node) to assert control or priority over others.
- **Linear Hierarchy**: A strict order: A > B > C > D...
- **Nonlinear/Networked Hierarchy**: More complex relationships; e.g., A > B, B > C, but C > A (circular dominance).
- **Matrix Representation**: Dominance can be represented using matrices or directed graphs.

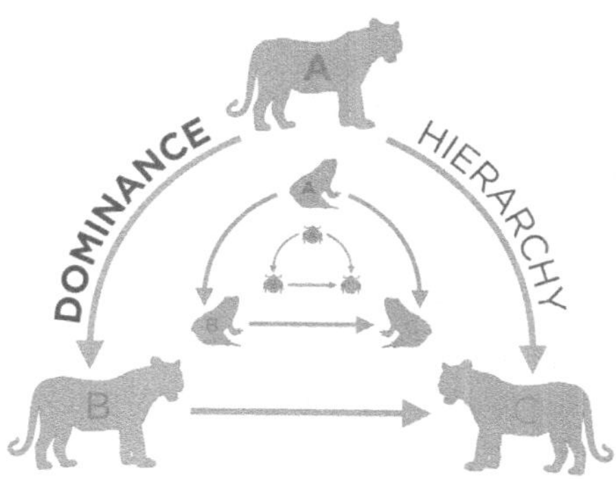

Third-Party Records **:**Third-Party Records refers to data or metadata collected from external sources—i.e., sources other than the primary user or platform. These records can play a vital role in understanding behavior, influence, and network structure, especially in areas like contact tracing, misinformation tracking, or brand monitoring.

Type	Example	Use
Mentions by others	User A is tagged by User B	Influence mapping
Shared content	User C shares a post originally made by User A	Virality tracking
Comment data	Comments *about* a person, product, or event	Sentiment analysis
Follower data	Who follows whom (even if the followed user never posts)	Network structure
Third-party app interactions	Facebook login data from an external quiz app	Behavioral profiling
Group membership	Who joins or interacts in shared groups	Community detection

Use Cases in Analytics

1. Influencer Detection

Third-party records (e.g. how many times someone is tagged, shared, or mentioned) can indicate influence level, even if the person isn't actively posting.

2. Epidemiological Contact Tracing (Digital)

In disease modeling via social media, if Person A is infected, you can identify third-party records:

Who tagged A at an event

Who shared a ride or location (via check-ins)

Who commented on A's recent activity

3. Brand Monitoring

Companies use third-party records to track what others say about them, not just their own posts.

4. Fake News or Misinformation Tracking

Tracing the spread of a post via re-shares, quotes, or comments involves third-party records to build a cascade map.

Sample Analysis Task (Numerical)

Scenario: You're analyzing the spread of a hashtag related to a protest. You find:

- 100 original tweets (from primary users)
- 350 retweets (from third-party users)
- 200 quote tweets (from third-party users)
- 120 mentions by users not involved in original posts

Insights: Third-party activity: 350 + 200 + 120 = 670 events

Ratio of third-party to original activity:

67 / 100=6.7 → high spread potential

Affiliation Network in Social Media Analytics

An affiliation network (also known as a two-mode network) is a special kind of network that connects two different types of entities—for example:

- Users and groups
- People and events
- Accounts and hashtags
- Influencers and brands

An affiliation network connects actors (e.g., people) to affiliations (e.g., events, hashtags, or organizations). It is a bipartite graph—two types of nodes, and connections only go between types (not within a type).

Citation Networks

Citation networks, traditionally used in academic research, can also be applied to social media analytics to track information flow, influence, and content virality. Unlike academic citations, social media "citations" include retweets, shares, replies, mentions, and hyperlinks—forming a dynamic, real-time network of digital influence.

Citation networks in social media analytics analyze the interconnected relationships between documents, such as academic papers, through their citations, revealing patterns of influence, knowledge dissemination, and research trends. These networks are constructed by representing documents as nodes and their citations as directed edges, allowing for the application of network analysis techniques to understand research landscapes and identify key players.

Applications:

Nodes and Edges: In a citation network, nodes represent individual documents (e.g., research papers, articles), and edges (or links) represent citations between them, indicating that one document references or cites another.

Network Analysis: Techniques like centrality measures (e.g., degree centrality, betweenness centrality) and community detection algorithms can be applied to these networks to identify influential authors, highly cited papers, emerging research trends, and clusters of related research.

Knowledge Discovery: Citation networks can be used to map the intellectual structure of a research field, identify key publications and authors, and understand how knowledge flows and evolves over time.

Social Media Integration: Citation networks can be combined with social media data to analyze how research findings are discussed and disseminated on different platforms, providing insights into the impact of research beyond academic publications.

Plagiarism Detection: Citation analysis, a key aspect of citation network analysis, can be used to identify potential plagiarism by detecting unusual citation patterns or duplicated citation sequences.

Community Detection: Partitioning citation networks into communities can reveal groups of researchers or publications that are closely related, helping to understand research specializations and collaborations.

Influence and Impact: Metrics derived from citation networks, such as PageRank or HITS, can be used to assess the influence and impact of research papers and authors.

Examples:

Co-citation Analysis: Examines the frequency with which two documents are cited together, revealing relationships between papers even if they don't directly cite each other.

Main Path Analysis: Focuses on identifying the most important links and paths within a citation network, highlighting the key intellectual trajectories of a research field.

Multiplex Citation Networks: Extend traditional citation networks by incorporating multiple types of relationships, such as citations, co-authorship, and social media interactions, providing a more nuanced view of research landscapes.

Methods & Tools for Analysis

1. Data Collection

- APIs: Twitter/X, Reddit, Facebook Graph API.
- Web scraping: For platforms without open APIs (with legal caution).

2. Network Metrics

- Centrality measures:
- Degree centrality: Most cited users/posts.
- Betweenness: Accounts bridging communities.
- Community detection:
- Modularity-based clustering: Finds echo chambers or interest groups.

3. Visualization Tools

- Gephi: Dynamic citation network graphs.
- Cytoscape: For large-scale social media data.
- Python Libraries:
- NetworkX (analysis)
- Tweepy (Twitter data collection)
- VOSviewer (for co-citation mapping)

3.11 Peer-to-Peer (P2P) Networks in Social Media Analytics

In social media analytics, a Peer-to-Peer (P2P) network refers to a decentralized structure where users (peers) interact directly with one another—without always relying on a central authority (like a platform algorithm or admin). These networks emphasize equal roles, direct communication, and collaborative behavior.

Social Media Context

Platform/Feature	P2P Aspect	Description
Whats App/Telegram	Messaging	Users communicate directly in groups
Reddit Threads	Discussion	Users respond in a thread-like, non-hierarchical way

Decentralized networks (e.g., Mastodon)	Federated sharing	Users interact across instances with no central server
Block chain-based social apps	True P2P	Data is stored/distributed among users, not by a company

3.12 Tools & Techniques for P2P Social Media Analysis

1. Data Collection Challenges

- No central API: Must crawl multiple instances/nodes.
- Encryption: Some P2P networks (e.g., Scuttlebutt) use E2E encryption.

2. Analytical Approaches

- Graph Theory: Model users/nodes and their connections.
- Consensus Algorithms: Study how information is validated in blockchain-based networks.
- Network Tomography: Infer trends from partial data (since not all nodes are visible).

3. Tools

- Block explorers (for blockchain-based networks like Steemit).
- ActivityPub analyzers (for Mastodon/Fediverse).
- IPFS & LibP2P (for studying content-addressed networks).

3.13 Recommender Networks

Recommender networks in social media analytics utilize social network analysis (SNA) to improve recommendation systems by considering user relationships and interactions. These systems analyze social connections, influence, and group behavior to provide more personalized and relevant recommendations.

"Recommender Networks" in social media analytics refer to AI-driven systems that analyze user behavior, content, and connections on social media platforms to suggest personalized content, people, ads, or communities. These networks combine recommender systems and social network analysis (SNA) techniques.

Recommender Systems: Suggest items based on user preferences (e.g., YouTube videos, Instagram reels).

Social Network Analysis: Explores user relationships, interactions, and influence (likes, comments, shares).

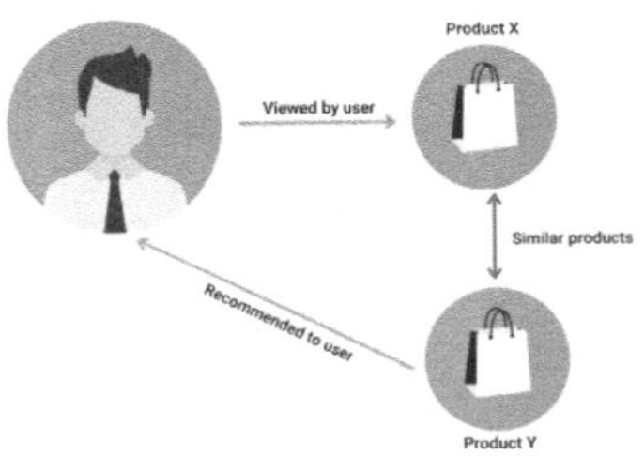

3.14 Recommendations in Social Media

Type	Examples
Friend/Follow Suggestion	"People You May Know" (Facebook/LinkedIn)
Content Recommendation	Reels, videos, posts (TikTok, YouTube)
Hashtag / Topic Suggestion	Twitter trending topics, Instagram tags
Ad Targeting	Personalized ads on Facebook, IG
Group/Community	Subreddits, Facebook Groups, Discord servers

Core Algorithms Used

1. **Collaborative Filtering**

   Based on user similarity (e.g., matrix factorization, user-user or item-item).

   Example: "Users who liked this post also liked..."

2. **Content-Based Filtering**

   Analyzes text, images, or video metadata (NLP, computer vision).

3. **Graph Neural Networks (GNNs)**

   Advanced models that process user-item interactions as graphs.

   Used in LinkedIn and Pinterest.

4. **Social Influence Models**

   Influence maximization, trust-aware recommendation.

5. **Hybrid Systems**

   Combine all above to improve accuracy and diversity.

Numerical Problem : You are analyzing a small social media platform.

You have data of 4 users and 4 posts. The matrix below shows whether a user liked (1) or did not interact (0) with a post.

Users \ Posts	Post A	Post B	Post C	Post D	Users \ Posts
User 1	1	1	0	0	**User 1**
User 2	1	0	1	0	**User 2**
User 3	0	1	1	0	**User 3**
User 4	0	0	1	1	**User 4**

Goal: Recommend **1 post to User 1** that they haven't interacted with using:

- **User-based collaborative filtering**
- **Jaccard similarity**
- **Top-1 nearest neighbor**

Step 1: Jaccard Similarity

Jaccard similarity between two users =

$$\text{Jaccard}(U_i, U_j) = \frac{|I(U_i) \cap I(U_j)|}{|I(U_i) \cup I(U_j)|}$$

Where I(Ui)= items liked by user i

User 1: {A, B}

Compare with:

User 2: {A, C}

1 /3 (only A is common, total unique = A, B, C)

User 3: {B, C}
1/ 3 (only B is common)

User 4: {C, D}
0/ 4=0 (no common likes)

Step 2: Pick Nearest Neighbor

Both **User 2** and **User 3** have Jaccard similarity of 1/3 with User 1. Let's pick **User 2** as the tie-breaker.

Step 3: Recommend a Post

User 1 hasn't liked posts: C, D

User 2 has liked: A, C

Post C is liked by User 2, and not yet by User 1.

So, recommend Post C to User 1

3.15 Biological Networks of social media analytics

Biological network analysis, which uses graph theory to model interactions between biological entities, shares conceptual and methodological similarities with social network analysis. Both fields analyze relationships between entities (nodes) connected by edges, representing interactions or connections. Social network analysis techniques like centrality measures and community detection are applied to biological networks to understand the structure and function of complex biological systems.

"Biological Networks in Social Media Analytics" draws inspiration from how biological systems (like neural, protein, or gene networks) function — using interconnected components, complex patterns, and self-organization. In social media analytics, these biological principles are adapted to model, analyze, and optimize user interactions, influence, content spread, and more.

What Are Biological Networks?

- In biology, networks represent complex systems:
- Neural networks: Neurons as nodes, synapses as edges.
- Gene regulatory networks: Genes regulating other genes.
- Protein-protein interaction (PPI): How proteins connect and function together.

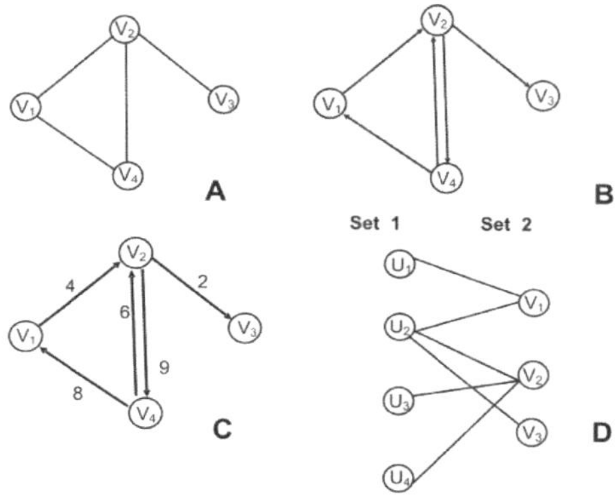

3.16 Biological Network Principles Used in Social Media

Biological Concept	**Social Media Analog**
Neurons	Users or posts
Synaptic connections	Likes, shares, comments, follows
Activation threshold	Virality or engagement level of content
Propagation	Spread of content (memes, news, hashtags)
Feedback loops	Comment threads, re-engagement patterns
Homeostasis	Network balance – avoiding information overload

Applications in Social Media Analytics

1. Information Diffusion Models

- Inspired by epidemiological models (like SIR in biology)
- Used to model:
- Virality
- Fake news spread
- Influencer impact

Example: Modeling how a tweet becomes viral similar to how a virus spreads.

2. Neural Network-Based Recommenders

- Deep learning models (CNN, RNN, LSTM) are inspired by biological neural networks.
- Used in:
- Personalized content feeds (e.g., TikTok)

- Predicting user engagement

3. Community Detection & Gene Modules

- In biology: genes form modules (clusters) for specific tasks.
- In social media: detect user communities or interest clusters using similar algorithms (e.g., modularity-based detection in graphs).

4. Graph-based Models (Bio-inspired Topology)

- Biological networks often have scale-free, small-world properties — just like social networks.
- Graph algorithms from biology (e.g., random walk, clustering coefficient) help:
- Detect influential users
- Model user behavior dynamics

Tools for Modeling Bio-Inspired Social Networks

- NetworkX (Python) – for graph modeling
- SNAP – scalable analysis of large networks
- Gephi – visualization of bio-social networks
- PyTorch Geometric / DGL – deep graph neural networks
- NetLogo – for simulating bio-inspired agent models

UNIT -IV

4.1 Social Network and Modelling

"Social Network and Modelling" typically refers to the analysis and representation of relationships and interactions within social structures using mathematical, computational, and graphical tools.

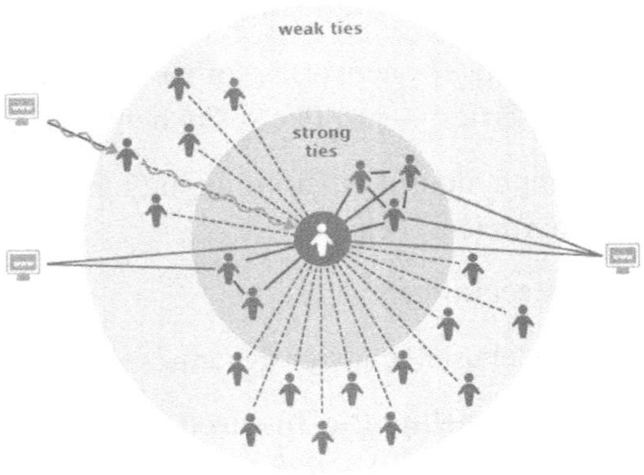

Social Network Modelling

Social Network Modelling involves building formal models to represent and analyze these networks. This often includes:

a. Graph Theory

- Social networks are modeled as graphs:
- Undirected Graphs (e.g., mutual friendships)
- Directed Graphs (e.g., follower-followee on Twitter)

b. Mathematical Models

- Random Graphs (e.g., Erdős–Rényi model)
- Small-World Networks (e.g., Watts-Strogatz model)
- Scale-Free Networks (e.g., Barabási–Albert model)

c. Statistical Models

- Exponential Random Graph Models (ERGMs)
- Stochastic Actor-Oriented Models (SAOMs)

d. Agent-Based Models

- Simulate behaviors of agents (people) and how interactions evolve over time

Applications

- Sociology - Studying friendship patterns, influence
- Epidemiology- Modeling disease spread via contact networks
- Marketing-Identifying key influencers
- Criminology - Mapping criminal networks
- Organizational Theory - Analyzing workflow and communication

4.2 Social Contexts: Affiliation and Identity

Social context significantly shapes individual and group identity. Affiliation with social groups, whether based on ethnicity, gender, religion, or other factors, influences how individuals perceive themselves and how they are perceived by others. These group memberships become a part of one's social identity, impacting self-esteem and behavior. Furthermore, social contexts, including cultural norms and socioeconomic status, play a crucial role in identity development, highlighting the dynamic and multifaceted nature of identity formation.

Affiliation: Social Connections and Belonging

Affiliation refers to the relationships and connections individuals form with groups, communities, or other individuals. It is rooted in the human need to belong and be part of something larger.

- **Group Membership:** Family, friends, ethnic groups, political parties, fandoms, professional organizations
- **Shared Interests or Values:** People affiliate based on common goals, beliefs, culture, or ideologies
- **Emotional Bonds:** Affiliation often includes emotional ties such as loyalty, trust, and mutual support

Examples:

- Workplace - Team members collaborating on a project
- Social Media - Following or joining specific communities
- Religion - Being part of a church, mosque, or temple
- Activism - Aligning with environmental or social causes

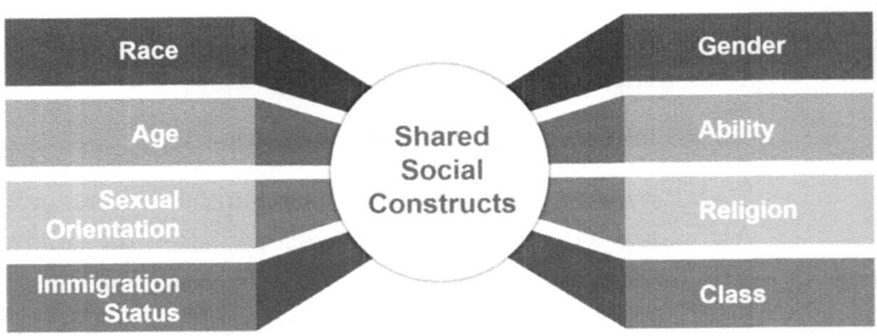

Identity: Who We Are in Social Contexts

Identity refers to the way individuals define themselves and are defined by others within a social framework. It can be personal, social, or cultural.

Types of Identity:

- Personal Identity: Unique traits, experiences, and personality
- Social Identity: Defined by group memberships (race, gender, nationality, religion)

- Cultural Identity: Shared language, values, traditions, and heritage

Interaction Between Affiliation and Identity

Affiliation and identity are interconnected:

- We often affiliate with groups that reinforce or shape our identity
- Our identity affects which groups we seek out or feel comfortable with
- Belonging to a group can enhance or constrain our self-expression

Example:

A student identifies as LGBTQ+ (identity), affiliates with an LGBTQ+ campus club (affiliation), and finds support and shared experience that further reinforces their identity.

Real-World Applications

- Marketing -- Brands target identity and group affiliations
- Politics -- Voter behavior influenced by group identity
- Education - - Identity-safe classrooms improve performance
- Healthcare -- Cultural identity affects treatment adherence
- Social Media-- Identity expression and group affiliation online

Numerical solution:

Problem: Affiliation Network Analysis

Scenario:

You are analyzing a university club network where students are affiliated with different clubs. Each student can belong to multiple clubs.

Given:

Students: A, B, C, D, E

Clubs: X, Y, Z

Club Memberships:

Student	Clubs
A	X, Y
B	X
C	Y, Z
D	Z
E	X, Z

Goal:

- Build an affiliation matrix
- Calculate the student-student similarity matrix based on shared club memberships
- Identify the pair of students with the highest affiliation similarity

Solution: Step 1: Affiliation Matrix (Binary)

Each row is a student; each column is a club. 1 = member, 0 = not a member.

	X	Y	Z
A	1	1	0
B	1	0	0
C	0	1	1
D	0	0	1
E	1	0	1

Step 2: Student-Student Similarity (Dot Product)

We compute a similarity score between each pair based on the number of shared clubs (dot product of binary vectors).

Example:

Similarity (A, B) = (1*1 + 1*0 + 0*0) = 1

Similarity (A, C) = (1*0 + 1*1 + 0*1) = 1

Similarity (A, E) = (1*1 + 1*0 + 0*1) = 1

Computing all pairs:

	A	B	C	D	E
A	2	1	1	0	1
B	1	1	0	0	1
C	1	0	2	1	1
D	0	0	1	1	1
E	1	1	1	1	2

Diagonal values (e.g., A with A) represent the number of clubs the student is in (for reference).

Step 3: Highest Similarity (Excluding Self)

The highest off-diagonal similarity score is 1, shared by multiple pairs:

(A, B), (A, C), (A, E), (B, E), (C, D), (C, E), (D, E)

These student pairs share one club. There's no pair that shares more than one club.

Interpretation:

- Students with shared affiliations (clubs) have stronger potential for social identity overlap.

- No student pair in this network shares more than one club, indicating diverse group identity affiliations.

4.3 Social capital

Social capital refers to the value derived from social connections and relationships. It encompasses the networks, norms, and trust that enable individuals and groups to achieve common goals and access resources. Essentially, it's the positive resources generated through social interactions and relationships.

Social Capital is the networks of relationships among people who live and work in a particular society, enabling that society to function effectively.

Types of Social Capital

Type	Description	Example
Bonding	Strong ties among similar individuals (family, close friends)	Support within ethnic or religious communities
Bridging	Weak ties that connect across diverse groups	Professional networking events, cross-cultural collaboration
Linking	Vertical ties with institutions or people in power	Access to government programs via local leaders

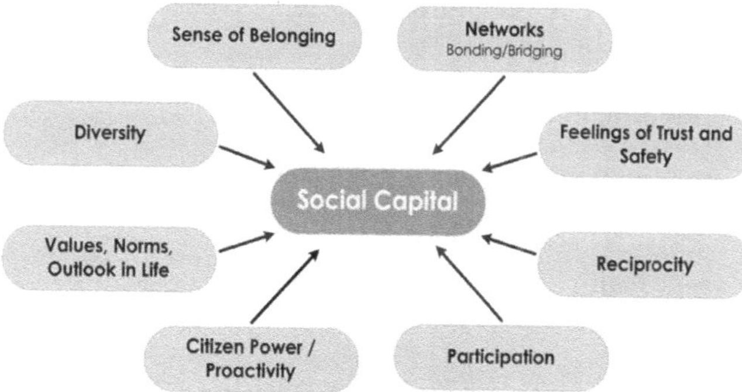

A. Bonding Social Capital

Definition: Strong ties between similar individuals (e.g., close friends, family, or tight-knit communities).

Function: Provides emotional support, solidarity, and a sense of belonging.

Example: A close group of college friends helping each other find jobs.

B. Bridging Social Capital

Definition: Weaker ties between diverse groups (e.g., acquaintances, colleagues, or people from different backgrounds).

Function: Expands opportunities, information, and resources beyond immediate circles.

Example: A professional LinkedIn connection leading to a job referral.

C. Linking Social Capital

Definition: Connections between individuals and institutions or those in positions of power (e.g., government, NGOs, or businesses).

Function: Provides access to formal support, policies, and systemic resources.

Example: A community leader advocating for better infrastructure from local officials.

Benefits of Social Capital

- Economic Opportunities: Job referrals, business partnerships, and financial support.
- Health & Well-being: Strong social ties reduce stress and improve mental health.
- Education & Knowledge Sharing: Mentorship, study groups, and access to information.
- Civic Engagement: Encourages voting, volunteering, and community participation.
- Crime Reduction: Trust and cooperation in neighborhoods lower crime rates.

How Social Capital is Built

- Networking: Actively forming professional and personal connections.
- Reciprocity: Helping others with the expectation of mutual support.
- Trust & Reputation: Being reliable fosters stronger relationships.
- Community Involvement: Participating in clubs, religious groups, or local events.
- Social Media & Digital Networks: Online platforms can strengthen (or weaken) social capital.

Problem: Measuring Social Capital in a Small Network

Scenario: You are analyzing a small professional network to estimate social capital based on how well-connected each person is and how important they are in facilitating connections.

Network:

There are 5 people in a professional group: A, B, C, D, and E.

Their connections (relationships) are as follows:

- A is connected to B, C
- B is connected to A, D
- C is connected to A, D, E
- D is connected to B, C, E
- E is connected to C, D

Goal:

Calculate two measures of social capital:

- Degree Centrality (number of direct connections)
- Betweenness Centrality (how often someone is on the shortest path between others)

Step 1: Degree Centrality

Person	Connections	Degree Centrality
A	B, C	2
B	A, D	2
C	A, D, E	3
D	B, C, E	3
E	C, D	2

Interpretation: C and D have the highest degree centrality, meaning they are more directly connected and can access resources/information quickly.

Step 2: Betweenness Centrality (Simplified Count of Shortest Paths)

We count how often each node lies on the shortest path between other pairs.

Let's simplify by counting these paths manually (real software like NetworkX does this more precisely).

- A is a bridge between B and C
- C is often in the path between A and E, B and E
- D is also a bridge between B and E
- B and E appear less often as bridges

Person	Betweenness Role	Betweenness Score (approx)
A	Between B-C	1
B	Minimal	0
C	Between A-E, B-E	2
D	Between B-E	1
E	Minimal	0

Interpretation: C again has highest betweenness, meaning it plays a key broker role, increasing their social capital.

Summary Table

Person	Degree Centrality	Betweenness Score	Social Capital (Combined Score)
A	2	1	3
B	2	0	2
C	3	2	**5 Highest**

			Social Capital
D	3	1	4
E	2	0	2

Conclusion: Person C has the highest social capital due to being both well-connected and a central facilitator in the network.

This means C has better access to information, influence, and resource-sharing opportunities.

4.4 Structural holes

structural holes refer to gaps in a social network where there is a lack of direct connection or communication between two or more individuals or groups. The concept, rooted in social network theory (notably by sociologist Ronald Burt), suggests that individuals who bridge these gaps can access and control information flows between otherwise disconnected parts of the network.

Structural Holes A structural hole is:

A missing tie between two nodes (people or groups) in a network.

A point of potential advantage for someone who connects these nodes.

Relevance to Social Media Analytics

In social media platforms like Twitter, Facebook, or LinkedIn, identifying structural holes helps in:

1. Influence Detection

Users bridging structural holes often have high social capital.

They are exposed to diverse communities, allowing them to spread information widely and quickly.

2. Community Analysis

Structural holes help reveal disconnected sub-networks or echo chambers.

Identifying brokers can uncover potential connectors between communities.

3. Viral Marketing & Campaign Strategy

Targeting individuals who span structural holes can maximize reach across otherwise isolated user clusters.

4. Innovation and Idea Diffusion

Those in bridging positions may introduce novel ideas from one group to another.

Helps understand how trends or misinformation spread.

Metrics and Detection Methods

In network analysis, you can detect structural holes using:

Betweenness Centrality: Measures how often a node appears on the shortest paths between other nodes.

Brokerage Roles (Gould & Fernandez typology): Types of bridging roles, such as gatekeepers, representatives, or liaisons.

Constraint Score (Burt's measure): Low constraint = high potential for spanning structural holes.

Tools Used

Gephi or NodeXL: Visualize and analyze structural holes in social networks.

NetworkX (Python): Code-based detection of brokers and network metrics.

Pajek / UCINET: Advanced SNA tools for researchers.

PROBLEM STATEMENT : Consider a directed social network on Twitter with 4 users: A, B, C, D. Their interactions (retweets or mentions) are represented as follows:

From	**To**	**Frequency**
A	B	5
A	C	3
A	D	2
B	C	4
C	D	1

We want to calculate the constraint score of node A, to determine whether A spans structural holes.

STEP 1: Normalize A's Connections

We first compute the proportion of A's time spent with each contact:

A's total interactions:

5(B)+3(C)+2(D) = 10

pAB = 5/10 = 0.2 pAC= 3/10 =0.3 pAD = 2/10 =0.2

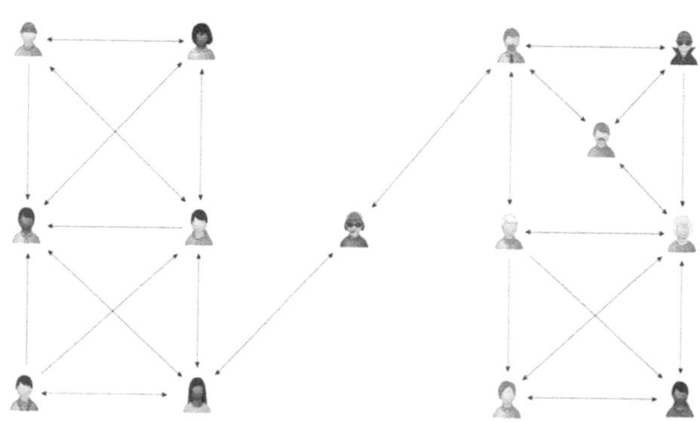

4.5 Structural balance

Structural balance in social media refers to how relationships between users or groups form stable or unstable triads, based on friendship or antagonism—essentially: "the enemy of my enemy is my friend" or "my friend's friend is also my friend." It originates from Heider's balance theory and is widely used in social network analysis to study community dynamics, polarization, and trust networks.

Concept of Structural Balance

In a signed network (where relationships are either positive = friendly or negative = hostile), a triad (3 nodes) is considered:

✅ **Balanced if:**

All three ties are positive (everyone is friends).

Two nodes are friends and both dislike the third (mutual enemy).

❌ **Unbalanced if:**

Two nodes are friends but one dislikes the third who is a friend of the other (creates tension).

All three ties are negative (everyone dislikes each other).

Real-Life Social Media Example

Imagine three Twitter users:

- A likes B (+)
- B likes C (+)
- A dislikes C (−)

This triad is unbalanced. If A and B are friends, and B and C are friends, but A hates C, it creates cognitive dissonance or potential conflict.

Over time, unbalanced triads in social networks tend to evolve into balanced ones (e.g., A might soften their stance toward C or distance from B).

4.6 Predictive Modeling

Social media has evolved into a dynamic platform where billions of users generate a colossal amount of data every second. The realm of social media predictive analytics has emerged as a game-changer, offering businesses unprecedented insights into user behavior and trends. In this article, we will delve into the intricacies of social media predictive analytics, exploring its working mechanisms, key components, benefits, challenges, and future trends.

Social media predictive analytics involves the use of advanced technologies and algorithms to analyze patterns, trends, and user behavior on social media platforms. It goes beyond hindsight analysis, enabling businesses to make informed decisions based on predictive modeling.

Predictive modeling uses algorithms to analyze past and present data (like posts, likes, shares, comments, and sentiment) to predict future outcomes — such as:

- What content will go viral?
- Which users are likely to churn?
- What are customers likely to say about a brand next month?
- Will engagement rise or fall?

Significance in Today's Digital Landscape

In an era where data reigns supreme, the ability to forecast trends and user actions provides businesses with a competitive edge. Social media predictive analytics empowers organizations to anticipate customer needs, refine marketing strategies, and stay ahead of the curve.

How Social Media Predictive Analytics Works

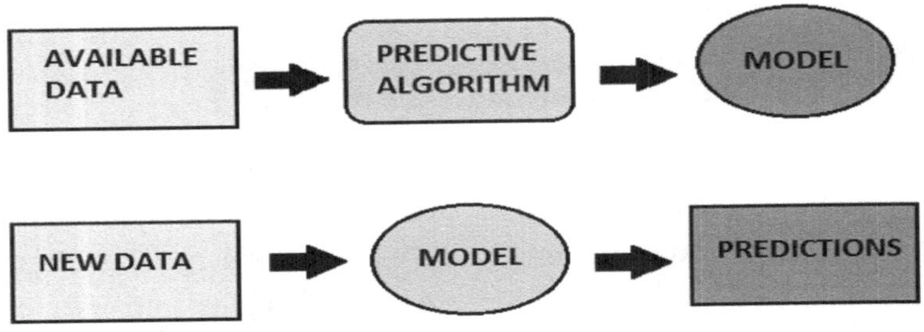

1. Data Collection and Integration

The foundation of predictive analytics lies in robust data collection. Social media platforms gather data on user interactions, preferences, and engagement metrics. Integration of this diverse data sets the stage for meaningful analysis.

2. Machine Learning Algorithms

Sophisticated machine learning algorithms process the integrated data, identifying patterns and correlations. These algorithms continuously learn and adapt, ensuring the accuracy of predictions over time.

3. Predictive Modeling

The culmination of data analysis and machine learning results in predictive models. These models forecast future trends, user behavior, and potential outcomes, providing actionable insights for businesses.

Sentiment	Definition	Example
Positive	Customer expresses a positive opinion or emotion	"I love the new product!"
Negative	Customer expresses a negative opinion or	"I'm so disappointed

	emotion	with the service."
Neutral	Customer expresses a neutral opinion or emotion	"The product is okay, I guess."

Key Components of Social Analytics

1. User Engagement Metrics

Understanding how users engage with content is crucial. Predictive analytics dissects metrics such as likes, shares, and comments, offering a comprehensive view of content performance.

2. Sentiment Analysis

Predictive analytics tools go beyond quantitative metrics, incorporating sentiment analysis to gauge the emotional response of users. This insight is invaluable for refining marketing messages and brand perception.

3. Trend Analysis

Identifying emerging trends allows businesses to capitalize on opportunities before they peak. Predictive analytics excels in trend analysis, offering a proactive approach to market dynamics.

Benefits of Utilizing Social Predictive Analytics

1. Improved Marketing Strategies

Predictive analytics enables targeted marketing by identifying segments with higher conversion probabilities. This precision enhances the efficiency of marketing campaigns and maximizes return on investment.

2. Enhanced Customer Engagement

Understanding user preferences and behavior allows businesses to tailor content and engagement strategies. This personalized approach fosters stronger connections with the audience.

3. Competitive Advantage

Businesses leveraging predictive analytics gain a competitive edge by staying ahead of industry trends and consumer preferences. This foresight enables proactive decision-making and adaptability.

Challenges

1. Data Privacy Concerns

The collection and use of user data raise ethical and privacy concerns. Striking a balance between data-driven insights and user privacy is a challenge that businesses must navigate.

2. Accuracy of Predictions

Predictive models are only as good as the data they analyze. Ensuring data accuracy and relevance is pivotal to the success of social media predictive analytics.

3. Interpretation of Results

Understanding and effectively interpreting predictive analytics results require a combination of technical expertise and industry knowledge. Bridging this gap is essential for actionable insights.

Future Trends

1. Integration of AI and Predictive Analytics

The fusion of artificial intelligence and predictive analytics is poised to revolutionize the field. AI-driven algorithms enhance the accuracy and depth of predictive models.

2. Emerging Technologies in the Field

Advancements in data processing, cloud computing, and machine learning algorithms are shaping the future of social media predictive analytics. Businesses must stay abreast of these developments to remain competitive.

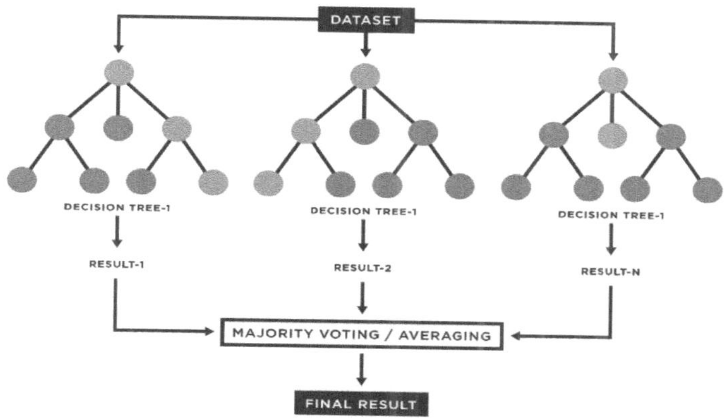

Industries Benefiting from Social Media Predictive Analytics

1. E-commerce

Online retailers leverage predictive analytics to recommend products, personalize shopping experiences, and optimize inventory management.

2. Healthcare

Predictive analytics aids healthcare providers in anticipating patient needs, optimizing resource allocation, and improving treatment outcomes.

3. Financial Services

Banks and financial institutions use predictive analytics to assess credit risk, detect fraud, and tailor financial products to individual customer needs.

Problem Statement:

A social media analyst wants to predict the number of likes a post will receive, based on:

The number of hashtags used (X_1)

The number of followers the user has (X_2)

Objective:

Build a regression model and predict the number of likes for a post with:

- 4 hashtags
- 1600 followers

Dataset

ID	Hashtags (X_1)	Followers (X_2)	Likes (Y)
1	3	1000	150
2	5	1500	250
3	2	1200	170
4	4	2000	300
5	1	800	100

Step 1: Linear Regression Model

$$Y=b_0+b_1X_1+b_2X_2$$

$b_0=17.33$, $b_1=11.67$, $b_2=0.1067$

Step 2: Prediction

Let's use the model to predict likes for:

- Hashtags (X_1) = 4
- Followers (X_2) = 1600

$$Y=17.33+11.67(4)+0.1067(1600)$$

$$Y=17.33+46.68+170.72=234.73$$

Predicted Likes: ~235

4.7 Descriptive Modeling

Descriptive modeling in social media analytics involves analyzing historical data to understand what has already happened on social media platforms. It focuses on summarizing and interpreting past events to identify trends, patterns, and anomalies, providing a foundation for future strategies.

Descriptive modeling focuses on summarizing and interpreting historical and real-time social media data to uncover patterns, trends, and relationships—without making future predictions (unlike predictive modeling). It helps answer questions like:

- What happened?
- How did users behave?
- What are the key trends and correlations?

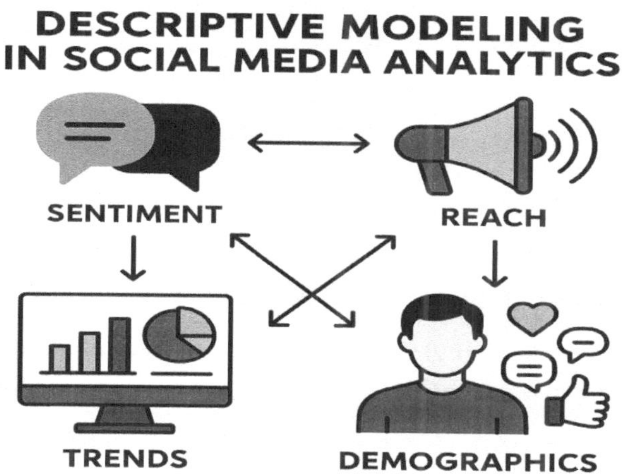

Elements include:

Sentiment Analysis: Understanding public mood by categorizing social media posts as positive, negative, or neutral.

Audience Demographics: Analyzing user attributes like age, gender, location, and interests.

Engagement Metrics: Tracking likes, shares, comments, and views to measure content reach and interaction.

Content Performance: Evaluating which types of posts (e.g., videos, images, text) perform best.

Trend Analysis: Identifying popular topics, hashtags, or events that generate high activity.

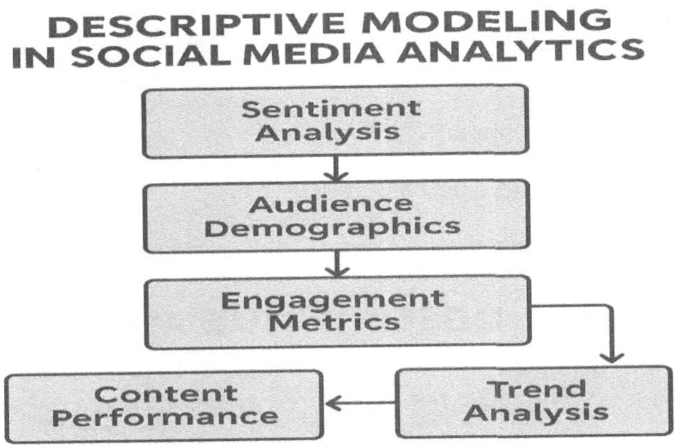

Components

Data Sources: Structured (likes, shares) and unstructured (text, images) data from platforms like Twitter, Facebook, Instagram.

Preprocessing: Text: Tokenization, stopword removal, lemmatization.

Network Data: Constructing adjacency matrices for graphs.

Multimedia: Tagging objects in images/videos.

Exploratory Data Analysis (EDA): tatistical summaries (mean engagement, sentiment distribution).

Visualizations (bar charts, time-series plots).

Descriptive Modeling Techniques: Clustering: Group similar users/posts (e.g., K-Means).

Topic Modeling: Extract themes from text (e.g., LDA).

Network Analysis: Identify influencers/communities (e.g., PageRank).

NLP: Sentiment analysis, keyword extraction.

Visualization:

Heatmaps: Show peak activity times.

Word Clouds: Highlight frequent terms.

Network Graphs: Visualize user connections.

4.8 Community/ anomaly detection

Anomaly detection in social media analytics identifies unusual or unexpected patterns of behavior, which can indicate malicious activity, spam, or other harmful events. This involves analyzing various aspects of social media data, including user interactions, content, and network structure, to identify deviations from established norms or patterns.

Anomaly detection in social media analytics helps identify unusual patterns that differ significantly from expected behavior. These anomalies can signal important events such as viral content, spam attacks, or system issues.

Common Types of Anomalies in Social Media:

1. **Sudden Spikes in Engagement**

   Example: A post suddenly gets 10× more likes than usual.

2. **Unusual User Behavior**

   Example: A user posts hundreds of times in a short period (possible bot activity).

3. **Hashtag Surges**

   Example: A rarely used hashtag trends unexpectedly

4. **Follower Growth Anomalies**

   Example: An account gains 10,000 followers overnight.

4.9 Techniques for Anomaly Detection

Method	Description	Example Use Case
Statistical Threshold	Set upper/lower bounds using mean & variance	Detecting spike in mentions
Z-Score	Measures how far a data point is from mean	Engagement rate anomalies
Isolation Forest	Machine learning technique for outliers	Detecting bot clusters
Time-Series Analysis	Analyzing trends over time for deviations	Traffic or trend monitoring
Clustering (DBSCAN)	Identifies dense regions vs. outliers	Community anomaly spotting

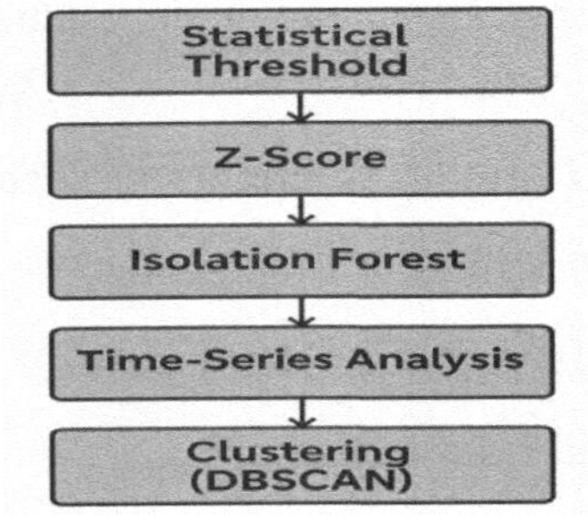

4.10 Facebook Analytics

Facebook Analytics is a tool provided by Meta to help businesses and individuals track and analyze user interactions on Facebook. While Facebook officially retired its standalone Analytics tool in 2021, many of its features have been integrated into Meta's broader tools such as Meta Business Suite and Facebook Insights.

Key Components of Facebook Analytics

Feature	**Description**
Page Insights	Data on page views, likes, reach, engagement
Audience Demographics	Information on followers: age, gender, location
Content Performance	Post reach, impressions, reactions, comments, shares
Funnel Analysis	Tracking user paths (in integrated apps/websites)
Retention Metrics	Measuring how many users return after first visit
Custom Events	Tracking specific user actions like clicks or sign-ups

Facebook Analytics Techniques

A. Descriptive Analytics

- Trend Analysis: Track post performance over time.
- Audience Segmentation: Group users by behavior (e.g., frequent engagers).
- Sentiment Analysis: Use NLP to classify comments (positive/negative/neutral).

B. Predictive Analytics

Engagement Forecasting:

Use time-series models (ARIMA, Prophet) to predict future post performance.

Churn Prediction:

Identify users likely to unfollow using logistic regression.

C. Advanced Techniques

- Network Analysis:
- Map interactions (comments, shares) to identify key influencers.
- Anomaly Detection:
- Flag fake accounts/bots using Isolation Forests.

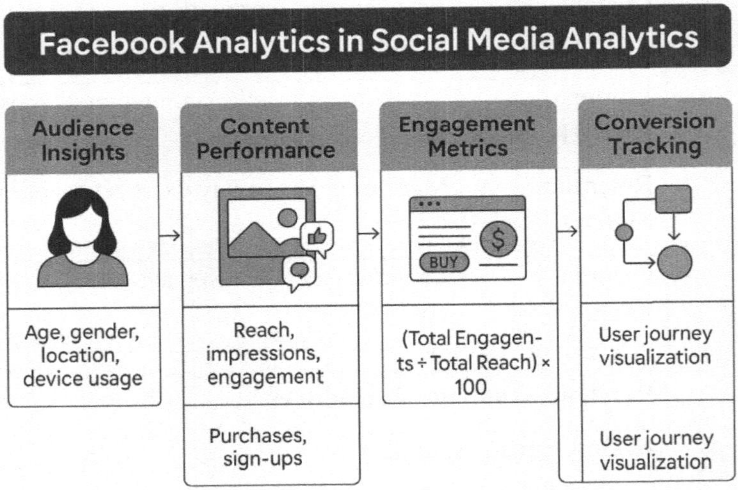

Challenges in Facebook Analytics

- Algorithm Changes: Frequent updates affect organic reach.
- Data Privacy: Limited access due to GDPR/Facebook policies.
- Fake Engagement: Distinguishing bots from real users.

4.11 Facebook Analytics by demographics

Facebook Analytics provides demographic data about your audience through its Insights feature, accessible within your Facebook Page's professional dashboard or Meta Business Suite. This allows you to understand the age, gender, location, and language of your page followers. This information can be crucial for tailoring content and ad campaigns to resonate with your target audience.

1. Facebook is the third most-visited website behind Google and YouTube as of 2025. This puts Meta's mainstay network ahead of other leading platforms like TikTok and Instagram.
2. The platform boasts 3.06 billion active users every month. This makes Facebook the most used social media platform worldwide.
3. In 2024, Facebook's total ad revenue amounted to $164.5 billion, up from $134 billion the previous year.
4. 44% of Facebook users interact with brand content on the network at least once a day
5. 40% of Facebook's user base actively shop on Facebook marketplace

Networks consumers have a profile on

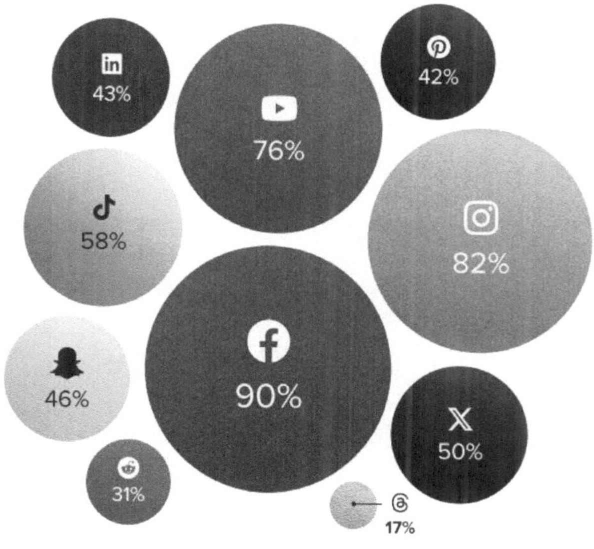

Top social media channels for customer care

Gen Z	Millennials	Gen X	Baby Boomers
Instagram 72%	Facebook 71%	Facebook 72%	Facebook 79%
TikTok 62%	Instagram 62%	Instagram 49%	YouTube 34%
Facebook 47%	X 29.5%	YouTube 41%	Instagram 31%

key parameters offered by Facebook Analytics:

- **Page Views:** The number of times your Facebook Page has been viewed.
- **Page Likes:** The number of people who have liked your Facebook Page.
- **Post Reach:** The number of unique individuals who have seen your posts.
- **Post Engagement:** The number of interactions (likes, comments, shares) your posts receive.

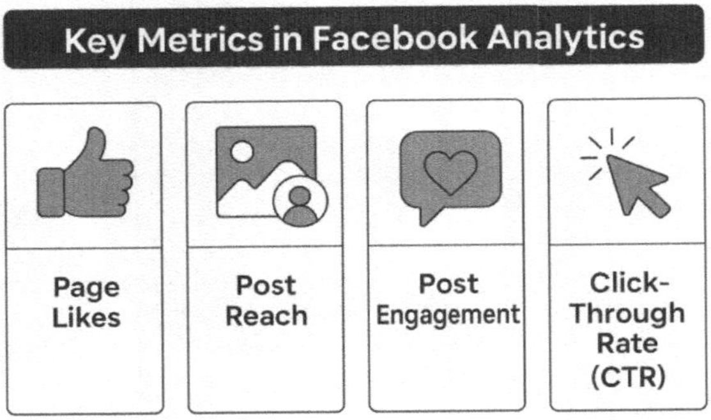

- **Impressions:** The total number of times your content, including posts and ads, is displayed.
- **Click-through Rate (CTR):** The percentage of people who clicked on a link in your post or ad after seeing it.
- **Conversion Rate:** The percentage of users who completed a desired action, such as making a purchase or signing up, after interacting with your content or ads.
- **Referral Traffic:** The number of visits to your website or app that originated from Facebook.
- **Demographics:** Information about the age, gender, location, and interests of your audience.
- **Retention:** The percentage of users who continue to engage with your app or website over time.
- **Lifetime Value (LTV):** The estimated revenue generated by a user uring their

lifetime engagement with your business.

- **Custom Funnels:** A series of steps that track user interactions and conversions, allowing you to analyze the effectiveness of your conversion paths.
- **Segmentation:** The ability to segment your audience based on various criteria, such as demographics, behaviors, and interests, to gain insights into different user groups.
- **Event Tracking:** The tracking of specific user actions within your app or website, such as button clicks, form submissions, or video views.
- **Ad Performance:** Data related to the performance of your Facebook ads, including impressions, clicks, conversions, and cost per action.

4.12 Google Analytics

Google Analytics can be used to track and analyze social media performance by providing insights into traffic sources, user engagement, and conversions from social media platforms. This helps businesses understand which platforms are driving the most traffic, how users are interacting with their content, and ultimately, the effectiveness of their social media strategies.

Why use Google Analytics for social media

Holistic View: See how social media traffic interacts with your website compared to other channels (organic search, direct, email, etc.).

Conversion Tracking: Understand which social media platforms and campaigns drive actual conversions (sales, form submissions, sign-ups, downloads, etc.). This is crucial for proving ROI.

User Behavior Insights: Analyze engagement metrics like bounce rate, pages per session, and average engagement time for social media visitors to understand their quality and interests.

Content Performance: Identify which specific content pieces shared on social media lead to the most website traffic and engagement.

Audience Understanding: Gain deeper insights into the demographics and interests of your social media audience once they arrive on your site.

Optimization: Use data to refine your social media strategy, allocate resources effectively, and optimize campaigns for better results.

Google Analytics Tracks from Social Media

Traffic Sources: Identifies which social media platforms (e.g., Facebook, Instagram, LinkedIn, X) drive visitors to your website.

User Behavior: Analyzes what those users do on your site — pages visited, time on site, bounce rate.

Conversions: Tracks whether social media traffic leads to goal completions like sign-ups, purchases, or downloads.

2. Key GA Reports for Social Media

Acquisition > Traffic > Source/Medium: Shows specific traffic from social platforms (e.g., facebook.com / referral).

Acquisition > Social: Dedicated reports for social media traffic, showing networks, landing pages, and conversions.

Campaign Tracking: By using UTM parameters on your social media posts, you can track performance for specific campaigns.

3. Best Practices

Use UTM Parameters: Tag all links shared on social media using Google's Campaign URL Builder. Example:

https://example.com/?utm_source=facebook&utm_medium=social&utm_campaign=summer_sale

Set Up Goals and Events: Ensure that conversions important to your business are tracked in GA.

Monitor Assisted Conversions: Found in Conversions > Multi-Channel Funnels. This helps you see if social media played a role earlier in the conversion path, even if it wasn't the final click.

4. GA4 and Social Media

In GA4 (Google Analytics 4), the model for tracking has changed a bit:

Go to Reports > Acquisition > Traffic Acquisition for social media insights.

GA4 emphasizes event-based tracking, so setting up events like button clicks or form submissions from social traffic is key.

5. Social Media Insights Beyond GA

Google Analytics shows how social media impacts your website.

For engagement on the platforms themselves (likes, shares, comments), you'll still need tools like Meta Business Suite, LinkedIn Analytics, or third-party social analytics platforms (e.g., Sprout Social, Hootsuite).

Scenario: You manage a website and want to analyze how social media contributes to conversions using GA4 data.

Data Example:

Social Platform	Users	Sessions	Conversions	Conversion Rate
Facebook	5,000	6,500	400	6.15%
Instagram	3,000	3,500	180	5.14%
LinkedIn	1,500	1,600	90	5.63%
X (Twitter)	1,000	1,200	40	3.33%
Total	10,500	12,800	710	5.55% (overall)

How to Calculate:

Conversion Rate per Platform = (Conversions ÷ Sessions) × 100

Example for Facebook:
(400 ÷ 6,500) × 100 = 6.15%

Key Metrics Interpretation:

- Highest Traffic: Facebook.
- Best Conversion Rate: Facebook (6.15%).
- Overall Social Conversion Rate: 5.55% across all platforms.

4.13 Google Analytics Brief Implementation

Google Analytics implementation involves integrating the Google Analytics tracking code into a website or application to collect and analyze user behavior data. This allows website owners to understand how users interact with their online presence and make data-driven decisions.

step-by-step outline for Google Analytics (GA4) implementation on a website:

1. Create a Google Analytics Account

Go to analytics.google.com

Set up an account and a property (choose GA4 for new implementations).

2. Add Data Stream

Choose Web as the platform.

Enter your website URL.

Copy the Measurement ID (e.g., G-XXXXXXXXXX).

3. Install GA4 Tracking Code

You can implement it in several ways.

How to Extract This Data in GA4

Custom Report in Explorations

Go to Explore → Free-form report

Add:

Rows: Session source/medium (e.g., facebook / social)

Values: Sessions, Conversions, Revenue, Average session duration

Apply filters for social traffic.

Export to Google Sheets for Calculations

Click Export → Google Sheets and apply formulas for deeper analysis.

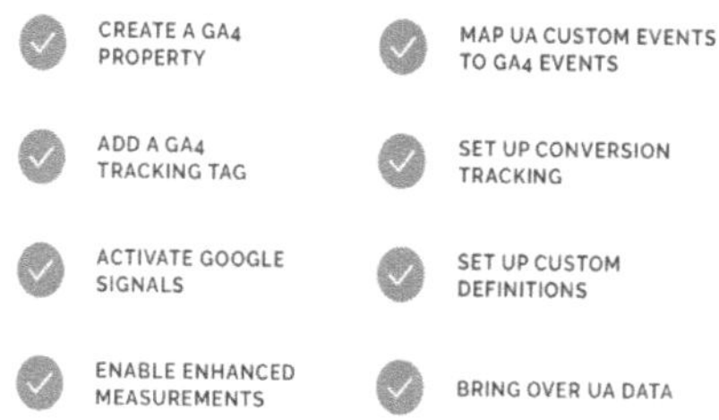

Google Analytics Performance Concerns

common Google Analytics (GA4) performance concerns businesses and developers often encounter, along with considerations for addressing them:

1. Page Load Speed Impact

Issue: Adding GA4 tracking scripts can slightly increase page load time, especially if multiple tags or third-party scripts are involved.

Solution:

Use Google Tag Manager to consolidate scripts.

Load GA scripts asynchronously.

Audit and remove redundant tags.

2. Data Sampling

Issue: GA4 applies data sampling when querying large datasets, potentially affecting report accuracy.

Solution:

Use BigQuery export for unsampled data.

Apply filters and shorter date ranges when exploring reports.

3. Data Latency

Issue: GA4 can take 24–48 hours to show some data in standard reports.

Solution:

For near-real-time needs, use DebugView and Realtime reports.

4. Event Limitations

Issue: GA4 has a limit on the number of unique events and parameters per property.

Solution:

Plan events carefully.

Consolidate similar events.

Archive unused event parameters.

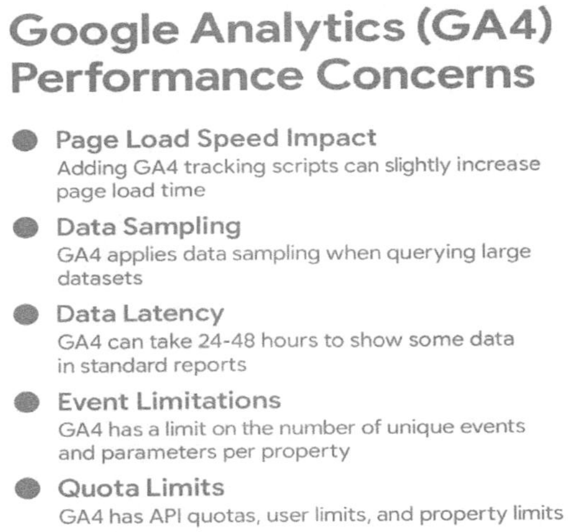

5. Quota Limits

Issue: GA4 has API quotas, user limits, and property limits.

Solution:

Monitor usage through Google API Console.

Request quota increases if necessary.

6. Privacy and Compliance

Issue: Compliance with GDPR, CCPA, and other data privacy laws.

Solution:

Use Consent Mode.

Ensure cookie policies and data anonymization are configured correctly.

4.14 Google Analytics Privacy Issue

Google Analytics (GA4) collects user data, which can raise privacy concerns under regulations like GDPR (EU), CCPA (California), and other global laws. Below are the main privacy risks and how to address them.

1. User Data Collection

Concern: GA4 collects user interactions, device information, and geographic data, which may include personally identifiable information (PII) if misconfigured

Consideration: GA4 prohibits sending PII such as names, emails, or phone numbers. You must actively avoid capturing sensitive user data through URLs or event parameters.

2. Data Storage and Retention

Concern: User data is stored on Google servers, often outside your country or region, raising jurisdictional privacy questions.

Consideration: Configure data retention settings in GA4 Admin → Data Settings → Data Retention (adjust to meet local compliance standards).

3. GDPR and CCPA Compliance

Concern: European and California privacy laws regulate how user data is collected and processed.

Consideration:

Implement Google Consent Mode to honor user cookie preferences.

Use IP Anonymization (enabled by default in GA4).

Display clear privacy notices and obtain user consent before tracking.

4. Third-Party Data Sharing

Concern: Data collected via GA4 may be used by Google for advertising or benchmarking.

Consideration: Review and manage data-sharing settings in your GA4 account, disabling features you don't want.

5. Cross-Device Tracking

Concern: GA4 uses Google Signals for cross-device tracking based on signed-in Google users.

Consideration: Activate Google Signals only if it aligns with your privacy policy, and inform users accordingly.

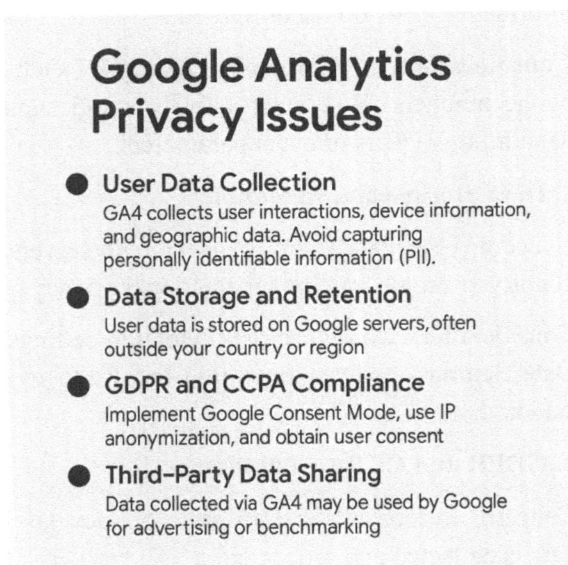

4.15 Google Website Optimizer

Google Website Optimizer is a free tool offered by Google that allowed users to run A/B and multivariate tests on their websites. It was discontinued in 2012 and its core functionality was merged into Google Analytics as part of Google Optimize.

Brief Overview of Google Website Optimizer:

Purpose: Help website owners improve conversion rates through testing different versions of web pages.

Key Features:

A/B Testing: Compare two versions of a page to see which performs better.

Multivariate Testing: Test multiple sections or elements simultaneously.

Integration with Google Analytics (before GA4).

☑ What Replaced It:

Google Optimize

Google Optimize took over from Website Optimizer and provided more advanced testing integrated with Google Analytics.

It was free for most users with an enterprise-level paid version called Optimize 360.

⚠ As of September 2023, Google Optimize has been officially sunset. Google has encouraged users to explore alternatives like:

Google Analytics 4's experiments features (limited)

Third-party tools: VWO, Optimizely, AB Tasty, Convert.com

UNIT –V

5.1 Processing and Visualizing Data in social media

Data processing and visualization in social media involves collecting, analyzing, and representing social media data in a visual format to gain insights and make informed decisions. This process helps in understanding audience behavior, tracking campaign performance, and identifying trends.

1. Data Collection and Processing:

Data Collection: Social media platforms generate vast amounts of data, including user activity, engagement metrics, and content performance.

Data Processing:

This involves cleaning, transforming, and structuring the raw data into a usable format for analysis. Techniques like data normalization are used to ensure consistency and quality.

Common Platforms:

- Twitter (X): via Twitter API (now X API)
- Facebook/Instagram: via Meta Graph API
- Reddit: via Reddit API (PRAW)
- YouTube: via YouTube Data API
- TikTok: mostly scraping, unofficial APIs

2. Data Visualization:

Purpose: Visualization transforms complex data into easily understandable visual representations like charts, graphs, and maps.

Benefits:

Improved Understanding: Visualizations make it easier to grasp patterns, trends, and outliers in the data.

Effective Communication: Visuals can communicate insights to a wider audience, including those without technical expertise.

Actionable Insights: Visualizations can highlight areas of success and areas needing improvement, guiding strategic decision-making.

Common Visualization Techniques:

Bar charts and line charts: Useful for comparing data points or showing trends over time.

Pie charts: Effective for showing proportions or parts of a whole.

Heatmaps: Help visualize the distribution and density of data.

Social network graphs: Visualize connections and relationships between users.

Tools:

Various tools, like those listed on Digital Agency Network, help create these visualizations.

3. Applications:

Social Media Analytics: Analyzing campaign performance, audience engagement, and identifying trends.

Marketing Optimization: Understanding customer behavior, preferences, and tailoring marketing strategies.

Content Strategy: Identifying popular content formats and topics to improve content creation.

Competitor Analysis: Monitoring competitor performance and identifying areas for improvement.

Risk Management: Identifying potential risks and addressing them proactively.

4. Best Practices:

Audience-Centric Design: Tailor visualizations to the audience's level of understanding.

Clarity and Consistency: Use clear and concise visuals, with consistent color schemes and fonts.

Contextual Information: Provide labels, titles, and data source information to aid understanding.

Interactive Visualizations: Incorporate interactive features like tooltips and filters for deeper exploration.

5.2 What is data visualization

It is the graphical representation of data by using graphs, charts, maps, and other visual elements that can be easily interpreted by everyone. In a way, it's a type of visual art that attracts people's attention and keeps their eyes on the most important message. Data visualization helps decision-makers understand difficult concepts or discover new patterns. The most common forms include:

- Bar charts
- Line charts
- Area charts
- Pie charts
- Histograms
- Scatter plots
- Heat maps

Bar charts are graphical representations that use rectangular bars to compare data across different categories. The length or height of each bar is proportional to the value it represents, making it easy to visually compare the magnitudes of different categories. They can be displayed either vertically or horizontally.

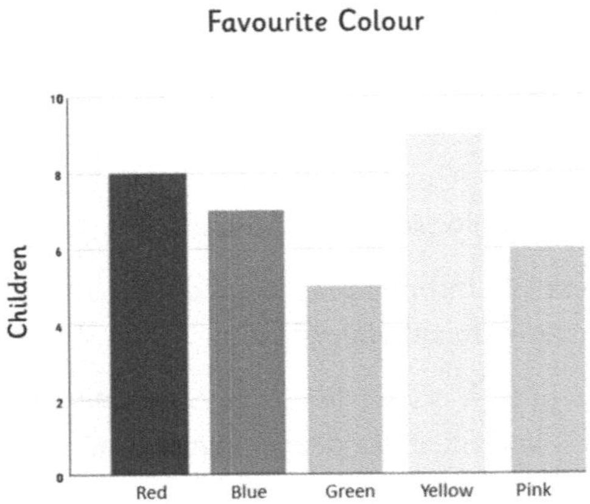

Features:

Categorical Data:

Bar charts are designed to display and compare data that falls into distinct categories.

Rectangular Bars:

Data is represented by rectangular bars, where the length (for horizontal charts) or height (for vertical charts) corresponds to the value of the category.

Proportional Representation:

The size of each bar is directly related to the value it represents, allowing for easy comparison.

Axes:

Bar charts typically have two axes: one for the categories and another for the numerical values.

A line chart, also known as a line graph or curve chart, is a type of graph that displays data points connected by straight line segments. It is commonly used to visualize trends, changes, and relationships in data over a continuous interval, often time. Line charts are particularly useful for showing trends in time-series data and for comparing trends across different categories.

Characteristics of line charts:

Data points: Line charts plot data points on a graph.

Lines: These points are connected by straight lines, creating a visual representation of the data's progression.

X-axis: The horizontal axis typically represents a continuous variable, often time.

Y-axis: The vertical axis represents the values of the metric being measured.

Trend visualization: The slope of the lines in a line chart indicates the direction and magnitude of change in the data.

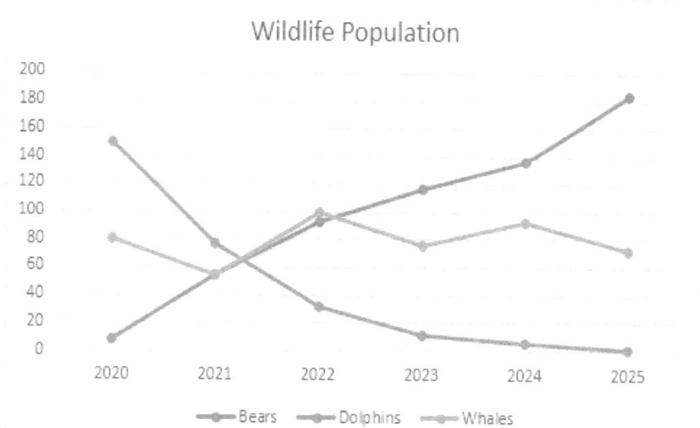

When to use a line chart:

Time-series data: Line charts are ideal for visualizing how a variable changes over time.

Trend analysis: They help in identifying patterns, increasing or decreasing trends, and overall trends in data.

Comparison of trends: Multiple lines on a single chart allow for comparison of trends across different categories.

Examples:

1. Tracking the stock price of a company over a year.
2. Monitoring the sales of a product over several months.
3. Analyzing the temperature changes throughout a day.
4. Comparing the performance of different marketing campaigns

Area charts are a type of data visualization that combines elements of line and bar charts. They display trends over time by plotting data points and connecting them with lines, while also filling the area between the lines and the x-axis with color or shading. This filled area emphasizes the magnitude of change and helps to highlight the total value across a trend.

Features:

Line Chart Foundation:

Area charts are based on the line chart, using lines to connect data points and show trends.

Filled Area:

The area below the line is shaded or filled with color, distinguishing it from a simple line chart.

Emphasis on Volume:

The filled area emphasizes the magnitude of the data values, making it easy to see the overall volume or cumulative effect of the data over time.

Comparison of Multiple Data Sets:

Area charts are often used to compare the trends of multiple data sets simultaneously, especially when showing how volumes change relative to each other over time.

When to use Area Charts:

Time-Series Data:

Area charts are particularly useful for visualizing trends and changes in data over a specific period, such as sales, revenue, or population growth.

Part-to-Whole Analysis:

Stacked area charts can be used to show how different subcategories contribute to a whole, and how their proportions change over time.

Highlighting Cumulative Effects:

When you need to emphasize the cumulative impact of data, like total profit or total users, area charts can be very effective.

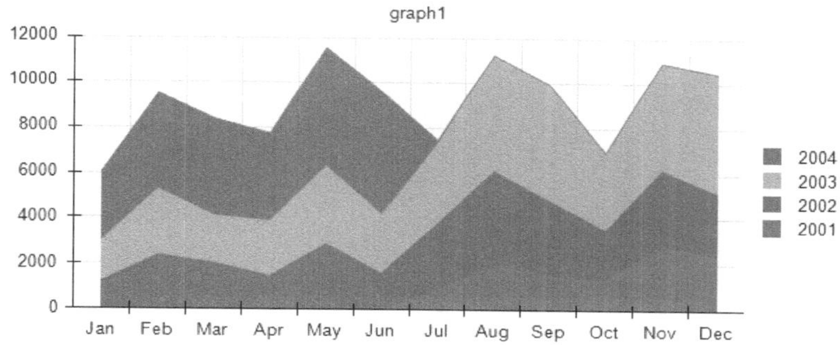

Types of Area Charts:

Basic Area Chart:

Displays multiple data series with filled areas, allowing for comparison of trends.

Stacked Area Chart:

Areas are stacked on top of each other, showing the contribution of each subcategory to the total.

100% Stacked Area Chart:

Similar to a stacked area chart, but the data is normalized to percentages, making it easy to compare the proportions of different subcategories.

A pie chart is a circular chart divided into slices, where each slice represents a proportion of the whole. The size of each slice corresponds to the quantity it represents, making it useful for visualizing the composition of a whole.

Here's a more detailed explanation:

Purpose: Pie charts are primarily used to show the relationship of parts to a whole, particularly when dealing with categorical data. They are effective for displaying percentages or proportions of different categories within a dataset.

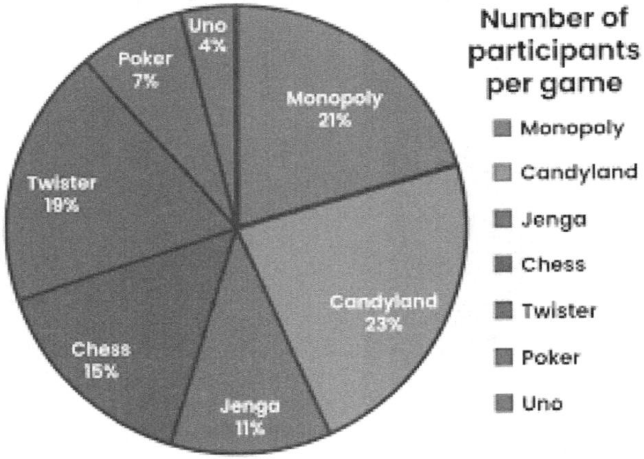

Features:

Circular Shape:

The chart is a circle, and each slice represents a portion of that circle.

Proportional Slices:

The size of each slice is directly proportional to the quantity it represents.

Categorical Data:

Pie charts are best suited for displaying data that can be categorized, such as different departments in a company or types of products sold.

Percentage Representation:

Slices are often labeled with percentages, indicating their contribution to the total.

When to Use:

Parts of a Whole:

When you want to show how different parts contribute to a whole, a pie chart is a good choice.

Limited Categories:

Pie charts work best when there are a limited number of categories (typically no more than 5-7).

Quick Overview:

They provide a quick visual overview of the proportions of different categories.

Limitations:

Too Many Categories: If there are too many categories, the slices can become too small and difficult to differentiate.

Comparison Between Charts: Comparing values across multiple pie charts can be challenging.

Not Suitable for Detailed Comparisons: For precise comparisons between categories, other chart types like bar charts may be more suitable.

Example:

A pie chart could be used to show the distribution of a company's expenses (e.g., rent, salaries, utilities) or the different age groups in a population.

A histogram shows the number of data points that fall within a range (called a bin). Unlike bar charts (for categories), histograms are used for continuous or numeric data.

When to Use Histograms in Social Media Analysis:

- Tweet lengths
- Number of likes/retweets per post
- Number of posts per user
- Time between posts
- Sentiment scores distribution

A histogram is a graphical representation of data distribution, particularly useful for showing the frequency of numerical data within specified ranges or bins. It uses bars of varying heights, where the height of each bar corresponds to the number of data points that fall within that bin's range. Histograms are particularly helpful for understanding the shape, center, and spread of a dataset.

features of a histogram:

Bins:Data is grouped into ranges called bins or classes.

Bar Heights: The height of each bar represents the frequency (number of data points) within that bin's range.

Continuous Data:Histograms are typically used for continuous numerical data, meaning data that can take on any value within a range.

No Gaps (usually): Unlike bar charts, histograms usually have adjacent bars with no gaps between them, as they represent continuous data.

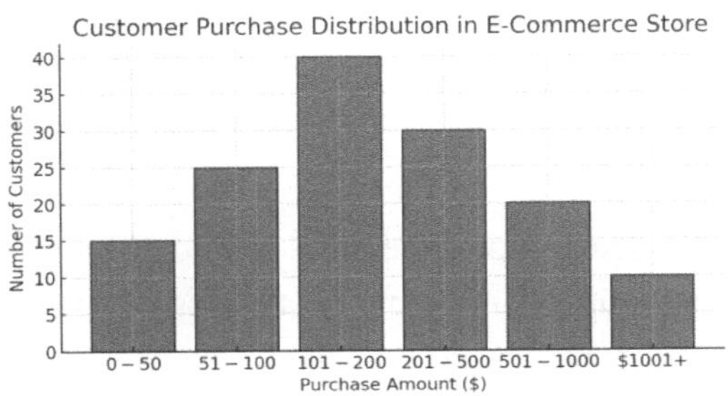

How to interpret a histogram:

Shape: The overall shape of the histogram (e.g., bell-shaped, skewed, uniform) can reveal important characteristics about the data distribution.

Center: The location of the peak or center of the histogram indicates the typical value in the dataset.

Spread: The width of the histogram indicates the variability or spread of the data.

Outliers: Gaps or unusually tall or short bars can indicate outliers or unusual data points.

5.3 Histogram vs Bar Chart

Feature	**Histogram**	**Bar Chart**
Data Type	Numerical (continuous)	Categorical (discrete)
Purpose	Show distribution of data	Compare categories
X-Axis	Numeric intervals (bins)	Categories (labels like names or hashtags)
Bars Touch?	Yes, typically (indicates continuity)	No, bars are separated
Use Case Example	Tweet lengths, likes per tweet	Most used hashtags, tweet count per user

- **Histogram** = "How is this numeric data distributed?"
- **Bar chart** = "How do these categories compare?"

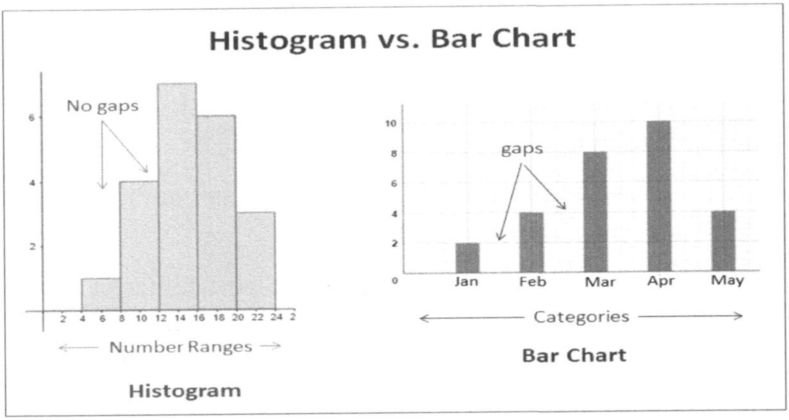

A scatter plot is a type of graph that displays values for typically two variables as a set of points on a two-dimensional plane . It is used to visualize the relationship between these variables, showing if they tend to move together (correlation) and how strong that relationship is.

aspects of scatter plots:

Two Variables:

Scatter plots are primarily used to examine the relationship between two numerical variables.

Visual Representation:

The data points are plotted on the graph, with one variable represented on the x-axis and the other on the y-axis.

Correlation:

Scatter plots help identify if there's a correlation (relationship) between the two variables. This can be a positive correlation (both variables increase together), a negative correlation (one variable increases as the other decreases), or no correlation.

Strength of Relationship:

The closeness of the data points to a line or curve indicates the strength of the correlation. If the points are tightly clustered around a line, the correlation is strong; if they are scattered widely, the correlation is weak or non-existent.

Form of Relationship:

Scatter plots can reveal the form of the relationship, such as linear (forming a line), non-linear (forming a curve), or no clear pattern.

Outliers:

Scatter plots can also help identify outliers, which are data points that deviate significantly from the overall pattern.

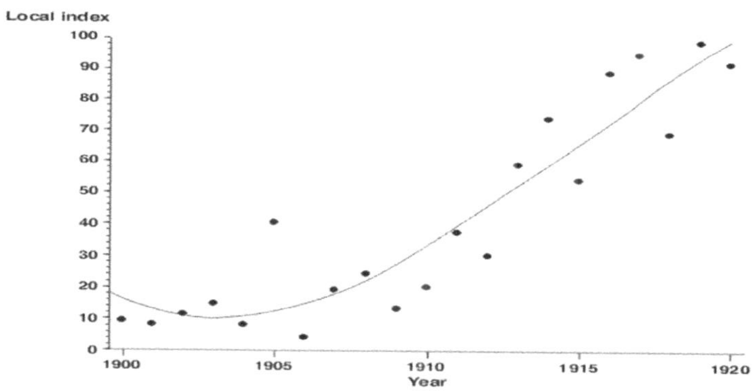

Examples of Scatter Plots:

Positive Correlation:

A scatter plot showing a positive correlation might display the relationship between study time and exam scores, where more study time generally leads to higher scores.

Negative Correlation:

A scatter plot showing a negative correlation might display the relationship between the number of hours spent watching TV and exam scores, where more TV time generally leads to lower scores.

No Correlation:

A scatter plot showing no correlation might display the relationship between a person's shoe size and their IQ, as these two variables are not likely to be related.

A heat map is a data visualization technique that uses color to represent values. It’s especially useful when analyzing patterns, intensities, or relationships across two dimensions.

When to Use Heat Maps in Social Media?

- Heat maps are excellent for visualizing:
- User activity across time (e.g. hour vs. day)
- Engagement levels by topic
- Correlation between metrics (likes, comments, shares)
- Geographic activity (with a geographic heat map)

A heatmap, also known as a heat map, is a data visualization technique that uses color to represent values in a matrix or grid. It helps to quickly identify patterns, trends, and outliers within a dataset. In essence, it's a visual way to display data where the intensity of colors corresponds to the magnitude of the values.

Aspects of heat maps:

Color Representation:

Heatmaps use color gradients to represent data values. Typically, darker colors (e.g., red, dark blue) indicate higher values, while lighter colors (e.g., green, light blue) represent lower values.

Data Visualization:

They are effective for visualizing large datasets and revealing relationships between variables that might be difficult to discern from raw numerical data.

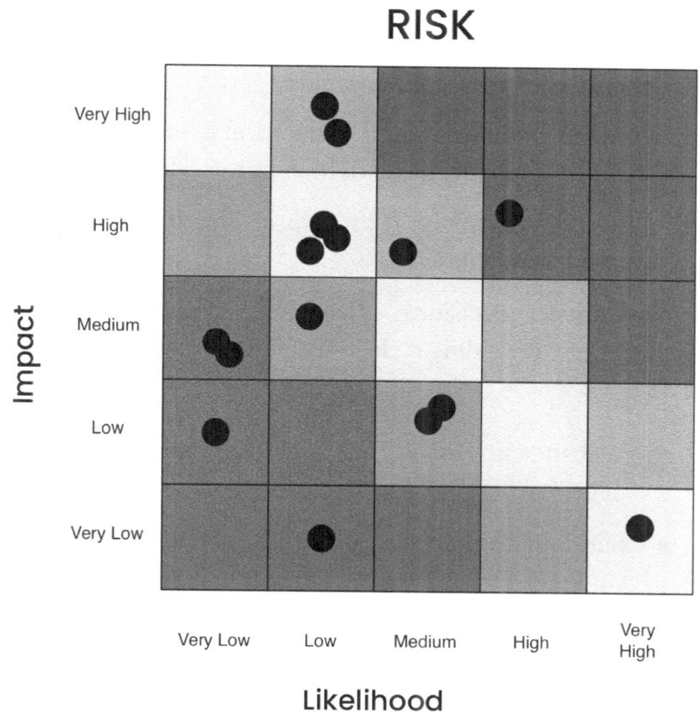

Applications:

Heatmaps have diverse applications, including:

Website analytics: Showing user behavior like clicks, scrolls, and mouse movements on a webpage.

Geographical data: Representing data distributions across different locations, such as population density or crime rates.

Financial analysis: Visualizing correlations between different financial assets.

Scientific research: Displaying gene expression patterns, protein interactions, and other biological data.

Risk management: Illustrating the severity and likelihood of different risks.

Benefits:

Improved understanding: Heatmaps make it easier to grasp complex data by highlighting areas of high or low activity.

Pattern identification: They help in identifying trends, clusters, and outliers within datasets.

Data-driven decisions: Heatmaps facilitate informed decision-making by providing a clear visual representation of data insights.

Examples:

- Website click maps: Show where users click most frequently on a page.
- Scroll maps: Indicate how far users scroll down a page.
- Election maps: Depict voting patterns in different regions.
- Gene expression heatmaps: Illustrate gene activity levels under different conditions.

5.4 Influence Maximization

Influence maximization in social networks is the process of identifying a small set of influential users (seed set) within a network to maximize the spread of information or influence through the network, often used in viral marketing or information dissemination campaigns. It's a core problem in social network analysis with applications in viral marketing, information diffusion, and public health.

Or

Influence maximization in social networks is a fundamental problem in social network analysis, marketing, and information diffusion. The goal is to identify a set of k influential nodes (users) in a social network such that, when these nodes are "activated" (e.g., given a product, idea, or message), they maximize the spread of influence through the network according to a diffusion model.

Problem Statement

A social network represented as a graph G=(V,E) where nodes V are users and edges E represent relationships or interactions.

A diffusion model (e.g., Independent Cascade, Linear Threshold).

A budget k: the number of users to initially activate.

Popular Diffusion Models

1. Independent Cascade (IC) Model

When a node becomes active, it has one chance to activate each of its inactive neighbors with a certain probability.

The process continues in discrete time steps until no new activations occur.

2. Linear Threshold (LT) Model

Each node is influenced by its neighbors, and it becomes active when the sum of influences from active neighbors exceeds a threshold.

Influence weights are typically normalized so that the sum for each node is ≤ 1.

Importance and Applications:

Viral Marketing:

Identifying influential users to promote products or services can lead to faster and more widespread adoption.

Information Dissemination:

Finding key individuals to spread information (e.g., public health announcements, event promotions) can enhance its reach and impact.

Disease Prevention:

Targeting influential individuals for vaccination or preventative measures can help control the spread of infectious diseases.

Algorithms and Approaches:

- **Greedy Algorithm:** A classic approach with a guaranteed approximation ratio but can be computationally expensive for large networks.
- **Heuristic Algorithms:** Methods like Degree Discount, PMIA, and CELF offer faster alternatives with varying degrees of accuracy.
- **Reverse Influence Sampling:** Techniques that leverage reverse influence sampling to improve efficiency.
- **Community Detection:** Algorithms that leverage community structures in social networks to identify influential individuals and maximize influence spread.
- **Particle Swarm Optimization:** Heuristic optimization algorithms inspired by social behavior in nature.
- **Network Representation Learning:** Using techniques like node embedding to learn representations of nodes that capture their influence potential.

Tools and Libraries

- NetworkX (Python): Graph processing and analysis.
- SNAP (Stanford): Scalable graph analytics.
- NetworKit, iGraph, Gephi: For visualization and large-scale analysis.

Challenges

- Scalability: Handling billion-node networks.
- Dynamic networks: Adapting to changes in network structure.
- Realistic models: Incorporating user behavior, time decay, or topic-specific influence.
- Fairness and Ethics: Avoiding bias in selection and misuse of influence strategies.

Example Graph

Assume we have a small directed graph G=(V,E)

Nodes: A, B, C, D, E

Edges (with influence probabilities):

A → B (0.5)

A → C (0.4)

B → D (0.3)

C → D (0.7)

D → E (0.2)

We want to select 1 seed node (k = 1) to maximize the expected number of activated nodes using the Independent Cascade (IC) model.

Find the node $v \in \{A,B,C,D,E\}$ that, when activated first, results in the maximum expected number of total activations.

Find the node

1. Start from A

Trial 1:

A active

A → B (success, 0.5) → B active

A → C (fail)

B → D (fail)

→ Active nodes: A, B → 2

Trial 2:

A active

A → B (fail)

A → C (success) → C active

C → D (fail)

→ Active: A, C → 2

Trial 3:

A active

A → B (success)

A → C (success)

B → D (fail), C → D (success)

D → E (fail)

→ Active: A, B, C, D → 4

Average spread from A = (2 + 2 + 4)/3 = 2.67

2. Start from B

Trial 1: B → D (success), D → E (fail) → B, D → 2

Trial 2: B → D (fail) → B → 1

Trial 3: B → D (success), D → E (success) → B, D, E → 3

Average = (2 + 1 + 3)/3 = 2.0

3. Start from C

Trial 1: C → D (fail) → C → 1

Trial 2: C → D (success), D → E (fail) → C, D → 2

Trial 3: C → D (success), D → E (success) → C, D, E → 3

Average = (1 + 2 + 3)/3 = 2.0

4. Start from D

Trial 1: D → E (fail) → D → 1

Trial 2: D → E (success) → D, E → 2

Trial 3: D → E (fail) → D → 1

Average = (1 + 2 + 1)/3 = 1.33

5. Start from E

No outgoing edges → influence = 1

Seed Node	Expected Spread
A	**1.67 BEST SEED NODE**
B	2.00
C	2.00
D	1.33
E	1.00

5.5 Link Prediction

Link prediction in social networks is the task of forecasting potential connections between individuals or entities within a network. This involves analyzing existing relationships and network structures to identify likely future interactions. It has various applications, including friend recommendations, identifying communities, and predicting future collaborations.

Concepts:

- Nodes: Represent individuals or entities within the network.
- Edges: Represent the relationships or connections between nodes.
- Link Prediction: The process of identifying potential future edges that might emerge in the network.

Methods for Link Prediction:

- Similarity-based methods: Use measures like common neighbors, Jaccard coefficient, or resource allocation to assess the similarity between nodes.
- Probabilistic models: Use statistical models to estimate the probability of a link forming between two nodes.
- Network embedding: Represent nodes as vectors in a lower-dimensional space, enabling the use of machine learning algorithms for link prediction.
- Community-based methods: Leverage community structure within the network to predict links.
- Temporal methods: Consider the evolution of the network over time to predict future links.

Example Applications:

- E-commerce: Recommending products to users based on their past purchases and browsing history.
- Social Media: Suggesting friends, groups, or content that a user might be interested in.
- Research: Identifying potential collaborators based on their research interests and publications.
- Security: Identifying potential criminal or terrorist networks.

Challenges:

- Large-scale networks: Analyzing massive social networks can be computationally challenging.
- Dynamic networks: Social networks are constantly evolving, making it difficult to predict future links accurately.
- Heterogeneous networks: Social networks often involve different types of nodes and relationships, making link prediction more complex.

Real-World Applications

- Friend recommendation (e.g., "People You May Know")
- Collaborator suggestion in academic networks
- User-item recommendation in bipartite graphs
- Knowledge graph completion
- Security: Detecting suspicious connections or behaviors

Common Link Prediction Techniques

1. Similarity-Based Heuristics

Operate on local or global network structure.

Metric	**Description**
Common Neighbors	(
Jaccard Coefficient	(\frac{
Adamic/Adar Index	(\sum_{w \in \Gamma(u) \cap \Gamma(v)} \frac{1}{\log
Preferential Attachment	(
Resource Allocation Index	Similar to Adamic/Adar but assumes equal resource allocation
Katz Index	Counts all paths between two nodes, penalizing longer paths

2. Matrix Factorization

- Factorize the adjacency matrix or similarity matrix into low-rank representations.
- Examples: Singular Value Decomposition (SVD), Non-negative Matrix Factorization (NMF)

3. Graph Embedding

Represent each node as a vector in low-dimensional space. Similar nodes (likely to form links) are close in this space.

Popular methods:

Node2Vec

DeepWalk

LINE

GraphSAGE

Then compute similarity (e.g., dot product or cosine similarity) between node embeddings.

4. Supervised Learning

Treat link prediction as a classification problem:

Features: Common neighbors, Jaccard, Adamic/Adar, etc.

Labels: 1 if edge exists, 0 otherwise

Train a model (logistic regression, random forest, etc.) to classify unseen node pairs.

5. Graph Neural Networks (GNNs)

Modern deep learning approaches that learn on the graph structure directly.

Examples: GCN, GraphSAGE, GAT

Often used with edge prediction heads for link prediction.

Python Tools

- NetworkX: Compute heuristic metrics (common neighbors, etc.)
- Scikit-learn: Train supervised models
- PyTorch Geometric (PyG), DGL: For GNN-based link prediction
- OpenNE, StellarGraph: For graph embeddings

5.6 Collective Classification

Collective classification in social networks is a machine learning technique that predicts the labels of nodes (e.g., users) in a network by considering not only their

own features but also the features and labels of their connections (neighbors). This approach leverages the relational structure of the network to improve classification accuracy, as nodes with similar connections often share similar attributes or labels

Why use it in social networks?

Homophily:

Social networks often exhibit homophily, where individuals tend to connect with others who share similar characteristics (e.g., interests, opinions, demographics).

Relational Information:

Collective classification methods can effectively utilize this relational information to make more accurate predictions about node labels.

Improved Accuracy:

By considering the network structure, collective classification can often achieve higher accuracy than traditional methods that ignore these relationships.

How it works:

Iterative Process:

Collective classification algorithms typically involve an iterative process. They start with an initial set of node labels (which might be partially observed or predicted using other methods).

Information Propagation:

In each iteration, the algorithm propagates information (label predictions) between nodes based on their connections and their respective attributes.

Refinement:

The algorithm refines the label predictions based on the propagated information, until a convergence criterion is met (e.g., the labels stabilize).

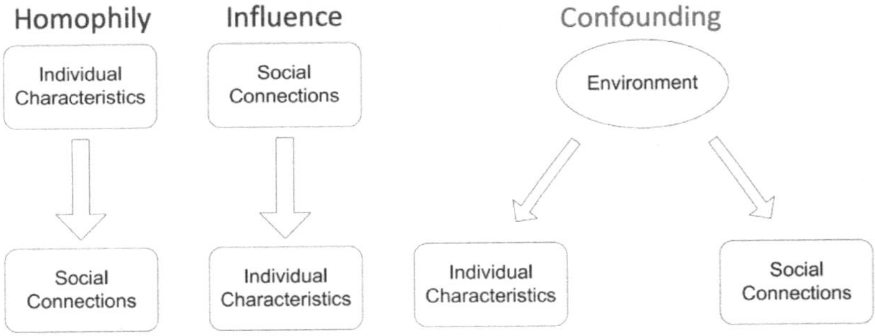

Examples of applications:

Predicting user attributes:

Classifying users based on their interests, political affiliations, or other attributes by considering their connections and the attributes of their friends.

Spam detection:

Identifying spam accounts in social networks by analyzing their connections and the content they post.

Community detection:

Grouping users into communities based on their interactions and shared interests.

Churn prediction:

Predicting which users are likely to leave a social network or stop using a service.

Challenges:

Computational complexity:

Collective classification can be computationally expensive, especially for large networks.

Scalability:

Developing efficient algorithms for large-scale networks is an ongoing research area.

Bias amplification:

If the initial labels are biased, collective classification can amplify these biases during the propagation process.

Method	**Type**	**Pros**	**Cons**
ICA	Heuristic	Simple, effective	May converge slowly
RNC	Heuristic	Easy to implement	Weak on noisy data
MRF / CRF	Probabilistic	Theoretically grounded	Computationally expensive
GNNs	Deep Learning	State-of-the-art accuracy	Requires more data and compute

Problem Setup

We have a small social network of 5 users:

```
  A(pro)     B(?)     C(?)
    \         |        /
     \        |       /
      \       |      /
        D(anti)
           |
         E(pro)
```

- Nodes: A, B, C, D, E

Known labels:

A = pro (1)

D = anti (0)

E = pro (1)

Unknown labels:

B = ?

C = **?**

Goal:

Use collective classification **to predict labels for** B **and** C.

Step 1: Initialize

We use the Relational Neighbor Classifier (RNC):
Predict a node's label as the majority of its neighbors' labels.

Step 2: Initial Guess (based on node features only)

Assume we have no meaningful features for now.

So we initialize all unknowns as 0.5 (uncertain probability):

B = 0.5

C = 0.5

Step 3: Iterative Updates (ICA)

We now iteratively update the unknown labels based on neighbors:

Iteration 1

Node B:

Neighbors: A (1), D (0), C (0.5)

Average of neighbors:

(1+0+0.5)/3 = 0.5 → stays at 0.5

Node C:

Neighbors: B (0.5), D (0), E (1)

Average of neighbors:

(0.5+0+1)/3 → stays at 0.5

Iteration 2

Let's say we now threshold:

If value ≥ 0.5 → label as **pro (1)**

If < 0.5 → label as **anti (0)**

We classify:

B = 1

C = 1

Final Predicted Labels:

Node	Label
A	pro (1)
B	**pro (1)** ✅

C	**pro (1)** ✅
D	anti (0)
E	pro (1)

Result

- Both B and C are **closely connected to pro users**, so they were classified as pro.
- This method **leverages the influence of neighbors**, which is typical in social networks where behavior or labels are correlated (homophily).

5.7 Applications in Advertising and Game Analytics

Collective classification is especially useful in domains where **relationships between entities** (users, items, or sessions) carry predictive value

1.Advertising Applications

Increase targeting precision, ad relevance, and conversion rates by leveraging social and behavioral patterns.

Use Case	**Description**	**Example**
User Attribute Inference	Predict missing user interests or demographics by looking at their friends or followers.	If many of a user's friends like "sports gear", infer the user may too.
Ad Click Prediction	Predict which users will click on which ads based on their neighbors' behavior.	If users with similar profiles or friend circles clicked an ad, the user is likely to click too.
Interest Propagation	Classify users into interest groups	Users engaging with tech blogs may pull

	collectively.	their connected peers into a "Tech Enthusiast" cluster.
Micro-segmentation	Build tight user clusters based on social behavior and classify them into actionable audience segments.	Helps with campaign targeting.

2.Game Analytics Applications

☑ Goal:

Improve player engagement, monetization, and retention by analyzing player behaviors in a network-aware way.

Use Case	**Description**	**Example**
Churn Prediction	Predict which players will quit the game by looking at behavioral patterns of their social group.	If most friends stop playing, the user might churn too.
Cheater Detection	Classify suspicious players based on known cheaters in their network.	Players closely connected to flagged accounts may also exhibit cheating behavior.
Play Style Classification	Categorize players (e.g., explorer, achiever, killer) based on in-game social interactions.	A player who often teams up with achievers may also be one.
Whale Identification	Predict which players will become high spenders by analyzing the spending patterns of their guild or friends.	Useful for early intervention or targeted offers.

Tools & Techniques	**Tool**	**Use**
	Graph Neural Networks (GNNs)	Learn from player/player or user/ad graphs directly.
	ICA / Relational Classifiers	Simple, interpretable collective classifiers.
	Stochastic Block Models (SBM)	Detect community-based patterns for targeting.
	Node Embeddings (e.g., Node2Vec)	Transform user interactions into features for downstream classification.

5.8 Collecting and visualizing social media data

Collecting and visualizing social media data is a common practice for research, marketing, and analytics in domains like political science, business intelligence, and network science.

Here's a complete breakdown of how to collect, process, and visualize social media data (e.g., from Twitter, Reddit, or Facebook).

Step 1: Collecting Social Media Data

Common Sources & Tools:

Platform	API / Tools	Notes
Twitter	Twitter API (v2) via Tweepy or Twarc	Great for real-time tweets, followers, hashtags

Reddit	Reddit API (PRAW)	Posts, comments, subreddits
Facebook	Facebook Graph API	Requires permissions; limited access
Instagram	Meta Graph API	Focused on business accounts
YouTube	YouTube Data API	Comments, likes, channel data

Step 2: Preprocessing the Data

Clean the text:

- Remove URLs, mentions, hashtags (or extract them for analysis)
- Lowercase everything
- Tokenization, lemmatization
- Remove stopwords

Optional:

- Language detection
- Sentiment analysis
- Named Entity Recognition (NER)

Step 3: Building a Social Graph

Use social connections (e.g., followers, mentions, replies) to build a graph/network.

Example:

Nodes = Users

Edges = Mentions, replies, retweets, or friendships

Step 4: Visualizing the Network

With **NetworkX + Matplotlib**

Step 5: Optional Analyses

Community detection: Louvain or Girvan-Newman

Centrality measures: degree, betweenness, eigenvector

Sentiment trends over time

Topic modeling using LDA

Step	Tool / Library
Data Collection	Tweepy, PRAW, Facebook Graph API
Cleaning	NLTK, spaCy, TextBlob
Graph Building	NetworkX, iGraph, SNAP
Visualization	Matplotlib, Plotly, Gephi
Analysis	Scikit-learn, Gensim, PyTorch Geometric

Example Projects

Hashtag co-occurrence network from tweets

Reddit community graphs by user overlaps

Influencer detection in Twitter follower networks

Toxic comment networks on YouTube

5.9 Visualization and exploration

Visualizing and exploring social media data involves transforming raw social media information into visual representations (like charts, graphs, and maps) to understand trends, patterns, and relationships within the data. This process helps in making sense of large datasets, identifying key insights, and facilitating informed decision-making.

Social media data visualization and exploration:

Data Collection and Preparation:

Gathering data from various social media platforms (e.g., Twitter, Facebook, Instagram) and cleaning it for analysis. This may involve removing irrelevant data, handling missing values, and transforming data into a suitable format.

Choosing the Right Visualization:

Selecting appropriate visualization techniques based on the type of data and the insights you want to convey. Common techniques include bar charts, line charts, pie charts, scatter plots, heatmaps, and network graphs.

Exploratory Data Analysis (EDA):

Using visualization to explore the data, identify patterns, outliers, and potential relationships between variables.

Storytelling with Data:

Using visualizations to effectively communicate findings to a specific audience. This may involve creating dashboards or interactive visualizations that tell a compelling story about the data.

Tools and Technologies:

Utilizing various software and programming languages like Python (with libraries like matplotlib, seaborn, and plotly), R (with packages like ggplot2), and specialized data visualization tools (like Tableau, Power BI, and Flourish).

Examples of social media data visualization and exploration:

Sentiment Analysis:

Visualizing the sentiment (positive, negative, neutral) expressed in social media posts about a brand or product using word clouds, bar charts, or time series plots.

Network Analysis:

Mapping social networks to understand relationships between users, identify influential individuals, and analyze the spread of information.

Trend Analysis:

Tracking the popularity of topics, hashtags, or keywords over time using line charts or area charts.

Geospatial Analysis:

Visualizing social media activity on a map to understand regional trends and patterns.

Benefits of visualization and exploration:

Improved understanding: Visualizations make complex data easier to understand and interpret.

Enhanced insights: They help in discovering hidden patterns and relationships within the data.

Effective communication: Visualizations facilitate clear and concise communication of findings.

Informed decision-making: Data-driven insights from visualizations can support better decision-making.

Type	What it shows	Tools
Network Graphs	User connections: mentions, replies, followers	NetworkX, Gephi, Plotly
Time Series	Tweet volume, sentiment, likes, etc. over time	Matplotlib, Seaborn, Plotly
Hashtag Clouds	Most common hashtags	WordCloud, matplotlib

Geolocation Maps	Where users are posting from	Folium, Plotly, Basemap
Topic Clusters	Topics or communities via clustering	Gensim + t-SNE/UMAP
Sentiment Distribution	Overall mood of tweets/posts	Seaborn, Matplotlib

Advanced Exploration

- Community detection (Louvain, Girvan-Newman) → Group users into clusters
- Centrality analysis → Identify influential users
- Topic modeling (LDA) → Discover common themes in content
- Embedding visualizations (t-SNE, UMAP) → Visualize tweet or user embeddings

Tool Recommendations

Purpose	**Tools**
Graph Visualization	NetworkX, Gephi, Cytoscape, Plotly
Dashboarding	Streamlit, Dash, Tableau
Interactive Maps	Folium, Kepler.gl, Plotly Geo
Text Analysis	WordCloud, NLTK, spaCy, Gensim
Topic/Sentiment Vis	Seaborn, matplotlib, pyLDAvis

5.10 Social Network and Web Data Analytics Methods

Social media and web data analytics methods involve collecting, analyzing, and interpreting data from social media platforms and websites to gain insights and improve business strategies. These methods help businesses understand their audience, track engagement, measure campaign effectiveness, and make informed decisions.

Social Media Analytics Methods:

Descriptive Analytics:

Summarizes past data to understand what happened, for example, calculating total followers, likes, or shares.

Diagnostic Analytics:

Examines data to understand why something happened, for example, analyzing why a particular post received a lot of engagement or why a campaign failed.

Predictive Analytics:

Uses historical data to forecast future trends and outcomes, for example, predicting customer behavior or sales trends.

Prescriptive Analytics:

Recommends actions based on predictive analytics to optimize performance, for example, suggesting the best time to post or which audience segments to target.

Sentiment Analysis:

Determines the emotional tone behind social media mentions, helping businesses understand public perception of their brand or products.

Cohort Analysis:

Groups users based on shared characteristics to track their behavior over time, revealing trends and patterns.

Social Listening:

Monitors social media channels for mentions of a brand, product, or competitor, allowing businesses to identify potential issues or opportunities.

Conversion Tracking:

Measures the effectiveness of social media campaigns in driving desired actions, such as website visits, purchases, or form submissions.

Network Analysis:

Examines the relationships and connections between users, influencers, and content on social media.

Audience Insights:

Gaining a deep understanding of the social media audience, including demographics, interests, and behaviors, helps tailor content and marketing strategies.

Content Strategy Optimization:

Analyzing content performance to determine what types of content resonate best with the audience, guiding future content creation.

Posting Schedule Optimization:

Identifying the optimal times to post content based on audience activity patterns.

Ad Performance Analysis:

Evaluating the effectiveness of social media advertising campaigns, including click-through rates, conversions, and return on investment.

5.11 Web Data Analytics Methods:

Website Traffic Analysis:

Tracking the number of visitors, page views, and bounce rate to understand website engagement.

Traffic Source Analysis:

Identifying the sources of website traffic (e.g., search engines, social media, referrals) to understand where visitors are coming from.

Conversion Rate Optimization:

Analyzing user behavior on the website to identify areas for improvement and increase the percentage of visitors who complete desired actions.

A/B Testing:

Comparing different versions of website elements (e.g., headlines, images, call-to-actions) to determine which performs best.

User Behavior Tracking:

Monitoring how users navigate the website, what content they view, and how they interact with different elements.

Path Analysis:

Analyzing the sequence of pages that users visit on the website to identify popular paths and potential bottlenecks.

5.12 Clickstream analysis

Clickstream analysis is the process of tracking and recording a user's journey through a digital platform, like a website, by analyzing the sequence of clicks or actions they take. It provides insights into user behavior, helping businesses understand how users navigate their site, interact with content, and ultimately optimize the user experience.

Clickstream analysis involves tracking and analyzing the sequence of clicks (or actions) a user takes while navigating a website, app, or digital service. It's an essential technique in web analytics, digital marketing, e-commerce, and UX research.

Element	Description
Session ID	Unique identifier per user session
Timestamp	When the action occurred
Page URL	Page or resource visited

Referrer	Where the user came from
Click Event	What the user did (click, view, scroll, etc.)
User ID / IP	Anonymized ID to track user behavior
Device / Location	Optional metadata for analysis

Techniques in Clickstream Analysis

1. Sessionization

Group user actions into sessions based on a time threshold (e.g., 30 min idle time ends session).

2. Path/Flow Analysis

Visualize and analyze most common user paths:

Entry → Browse → Product → Cart → Checkout → Exit

Tools: Sankey diagrams, Markov chains

3. Funnel Analysis

Track how users move through a defined process (e.g., product view → cart → payment).

4. Sequence Mining

Mine frequent sequences of clicks to discover patterns (e.g., PrefixSpan, GSP algorithms).

5. Clustering

Cluster users or sessions by behavior (e.g., fast browsers, deep explorers, single-page visitors).

6. Predictive Modeling

Predict outcomes (e.g., purchase intent, churn) using sequence features.

Key aspects of clickstream analysis:

Tracking user journeys:

Clickstream analysis records the sequence of pages a user visits, the links they click, and other interactions they make on a website or application.

Identifying user behavior patterns:

By analyzing these clickstreams, businesses can identify common paths users take, where they spend the most time, and where they drop off, providing insights into user preferences and pain points.

Optimizing user experience:

Understanding user behavior through clickstream analysis allows businesses to make data-driven decisions to improve website navigation, content presentation, and overall user experience, leading to increased engagement and conversions.

Various applications: Clickstream analysis is widely used in e-commerce, online learning platforms, and other digital businesses to understand customer behavior, improve marketing strategies, and optimize website performance.

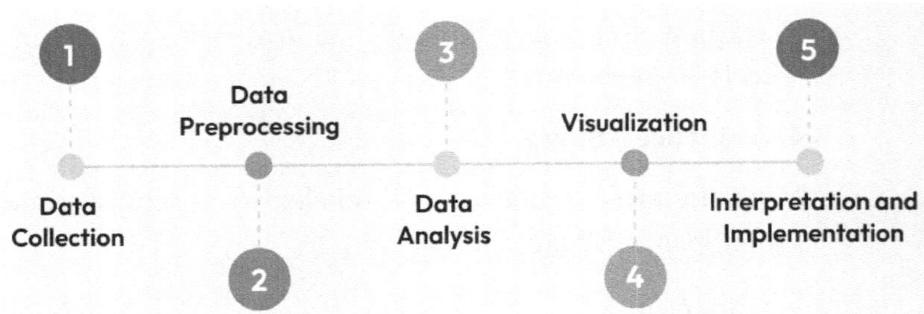

Problem Statement

An e-commerce site records user navigation through the following **4-step funnel**:

Home → Product Page → Add to Cart → Checkout

Here is the clickstream data collected from 1,000 users:

Step	Number of Users
Home	1,000
Product Page	800
Add to Cart	400
Checkout	100

We'll answer the following:

- Conversion rate at each step
- Drop-off count and rate between steps
- Overall funnel conversion rate
- Interpret the results

1. Conversion Rate at Each Step

Conversion rate from one step to the next is:

$$\text{Conversion Rate} = \frac{\text{Users at Next Step}}{\text{Users at Current Step}} \times 100\%$$

Calculations:

- Home → Product Page:
  $\frac{800}{1000} = 0.80$ → **80%**
- Product Page → Add to Cart:
  $\frac{400}{800} = 0.50$ → **50%**
- Add to Cart → Checkout:
  $\frac{100}{400} = 0.25$ → **25%**

2. Drop-off Count and Rate

Drop-off = Users who did not proceed to the next step.

Drop-off Counts:

Home → Product Page:
1000 – 800 = 200

Product Page → Add to Cart:
$800 - 400 = 400$

Add to Cart → Checkout:
$400 - 100 = 300$

Drop-off Rates:

$$\text{Drop-off Rate} = \frac{\text{Users Dropped}}{\text{Users at Current Step}} \times 100\%$$

- Home → Product Page:
  $\frac{200}{1000} = 20\%$
- Product Page → Add to Cart:
  $\frac{400}{800} = 50\%$
- Add to Cart → Checkout:
  $\frac{300}{400} = 75\%$

3. Overall Funnel Conversion Rate

From Home → Checkout:

\text{Overall Conversion Rate} = \frac{100}{1000} = 0.10 = \textbf{10%}

Only 10% of users who entered the site completed a purchase.

4. Interpretation

Step Transition	Conv. Rate	Drop-off	Drop-off Rate
Home → Product Page	80%	200	20%
Product Page → Add to Cart	50%	400	50%
Add to Cart → Checkout	25%	300	75%

5.13 A/B testing

A/B testing, also known as split testing or bucket testing, is a method of comparing two versions of a webpage, app screen, or other digital asset to see which one performs better based on a specific metric. It involves randomly assigning users to view one of the two versions and then analyzing the results to determine which version is more effective in achieving a desired outcome. This data-driven approach helps optimize user experience and improve conversion rates.

A/B testing is a method used to compare two versions of something to determine which one performs better. It's commonly used in marketing, product design, web development, and UX/UI design.

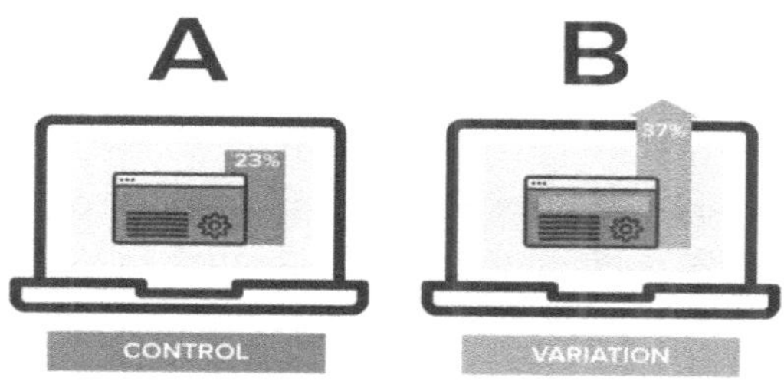

How it works:

1. Define a hypothesis:

Identify a specific element or design you want to test and form a hypothesis about how it will impact user behavior. For example, you might hypothesize that a different headline on a landing page will lead to more sign-ups.

2. Create variations:

Develop two versions of the element you're testing (A and B), where A is the original (control) and B is the variation.

3. Randomly assign users:

Divide your target audience into two groups, with each group seeing either version A or version B.

4. Track and analyze results:

Monitor key metrics (e.g., click-through rates, conversion rates, time spent on page) to see which version performs better based on your hypothesis.

5. Implement the winning version:

If the variation (B) performs significantly better than the original (A), implement it as the new standard.

Examples of A/B testing:

Website copy:

Testing different headlines, calls to action, or body text to see which resonates better with visitors.

Email marketing:

Comparing subject lines, email layouts, or call-to-action buttons to optimize open rates and click-through rates.

Mobile app design:

Evaluating different layouts, button placements, or on boarding flows to improve user engagement.

Benefits of A/B testing:

Data-driven decisions:

A/B testing allows you to make informed decisions based on real user behavior, rather than relying on intuition.

Improved user experience:

By identifying what works best for your audience, you can optimize your website or app to provide a better user experience.

Increased conversions:

A/B testing can help you improve conversion rates, whether it's sign-ups, purchases, or other desired actions.

Reduced risk:

By testing changes in a controlled environment, you can minimize the risk of implementing changes that might negatively impact your website or app

5.14 Online surveys

Online surveys are a popular method for collecting data, feedback, or opinions from

a specific audience over the internet. They're widely used in research, marketing, customer satisfaction analysis, product development, and UX design.

Components of an Online Survey

1. **Objective**
    - Clearly define what you're trying to learn.
    - Example: Understand user satisfaction with a new app feature.
2. **Target Audience**
    - Identify who should take the survey.
    - Example: Existing customers, first-time visitors, etc.

3. **Question Types**
    - Multiple choice
    - Rating scales (Likert)
    - Open-ended
    - Yes/No
    - Dropdowns
4. **Distribution Methods**
    - Email
    - Website pop-ups or banners
    - Social media
    - In-app prompts
    - QR codes or links in printed materials
5. **Survey Tools**
    - Google Forms (free, basic)
    - Typeform (interactive, sleek UI)
    - SurveyMonkey (robust analytics)
    - Qualtrics (enterprise-level)
    - Microsoft Forms, Jotform, Zoho Survey, etc.

Example Use Cases

- Customer Satisfaction Survey (CSAT)
- Net Promoter Score (NPS)
- Market Research Survey
- Employee Engagement Survey
- Product Feedback Survey

5.14 Web crawling and Indexing.

Web crawling and indexing are fundamental processes for search engines like Google. Crawling is the discovery of web pages and links, while indexing involves analyzing and storing the content of those pages for future searches. Essentially, crawlers find web pages, and the index stores the information needed to match user search queries with relevant results.

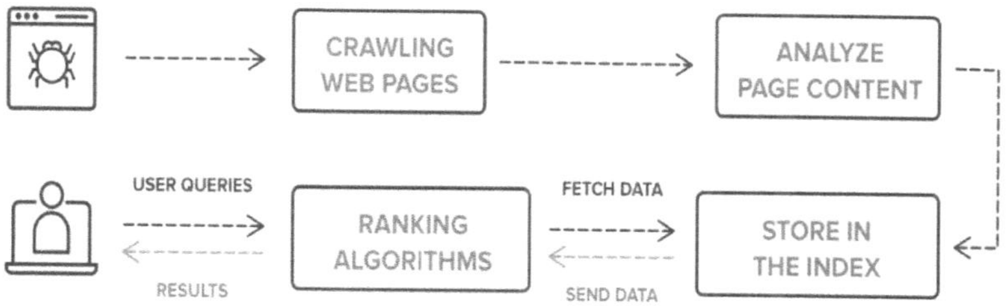

Crawling:

A web crawler, also known as a spider or bot, is a program that automatically browses the internet to discover new web pages.

Crawlers follow links from known pages to find new ones, scanning content, and collecting data.

This process helps search engines build a map of the web, identifying new content and updates to existing pages.

Web crawling is the process of automatically browsing the web to find and collect content (web pages, images, files, etc.).

How it works:

- Starts with a list of URLs (seeds).
- A crawler (or bot/spider) visits each URL.
- It downloads the page content (HTML, images, links).
- Finds all the hyperlinks on the page.
- Adds new URLs to the list to crawl next.

- Repeats this process at scale.

Indexing:

Once a crawler has visited a page, the indexing process begins.

Indexing involves analyzing the content of the page, including text, images, and metadata, and storing this information in a massive database called the search engine index.

This index allows the search engine to quickly retrieve relevant results when a user enters a search query.

Essentially, indexing is the process of organizing and storing the vast amount of information gathered during crawling.

Indexing is the process of storing and organizing the content found during crawling, so it can be retrieved quickly when a user does a search.

How it works:

- Crawler sends page data to the indexer.
- The indexer analyzes the content:
- Extracts text
- Identifies keywords, topics, and structure (like headings, links)
- Stores a summary in a search index (like a giant digital library)
- This indexed data is used to match search queries with relevant content.

In simpler terms:

Imagine the internet as a massive library. Crawling is like sending librarians to explore the library, discover new books (web pages), and make notes about them. Indexing is like creating a catalog for the library, organizing the books by subject matter (keywords) so that readers can easily find what they're looking for.

Real-World Tools for Crawling and Indexing

- Crawlers:
- Scrapy (Python)
- BeautifulSoup (Python)
- Selenium (for dynamic sites)
- Googlebot (used by Google)

Indexing Engines:

- Elasticsearch (popular for custom search engines)
- Apache Lucene / Solr
- Whoosh (Python)

Problem Statement

A search engine wants to crawl and index a group of websites. Here's the setup:

It starts with 10 seed URLs.

Each page contains an average of 5 outgoing links.

The crawler has a limit of 3 levels of depth (from the seed URLs).

The crawler avoids revisiting any previously visited URL.

After crawling, the system indexes only HTML pages, which are 80% of all pages discovered.

Q1. How many unique pages will be crawled (assuming no duplicate links)?

Q2. How many of those will be indexed?

Depth 0 (Initial seeds)

10 URLs

Depth 1

Each of the 10 pages has 5 outgoing links → 10 × 5 = 50 pages

Depth 2

Each of the 50 pages has 5 outgoing links → 50 × 5 = 250 pages

Depth 3

Each of the 250 pages has 5 outgoing links → 250 × 5 = 1,250 pages

Total Pages Crawled:

= Depth 0 + Depth 1 + Depth 2 + Depth 3

= 10 + 50 + 250 + 1,250 = 1,560 pages

Q1 Answer: 1,560 unique pages crawled

Q2: Pages Indexed

Only 80% of pages are valid HTML and eligible for indexing:

= 80% of 1,560 = 0.8 × 1,560 = 1,248 pages

Q2 Answer: 1,248 pages indexed

5.15 Natural Language Processing Techniques for Micro-text Analysis

Natural Language Processing (NLP) techniques offer valuable tools for analyzing micro-text, which includes short, informal text like social media posts and text messages. These techniques enable computers to understand, interpret, and extract insights from this type of data. Key NLP methods include tokenization, stemming, stop word removal, part-of-speech tagging, sentiment analysis, and named entity recognition.

Natural Language Processing (NLP) Techniques for Micro-text Analysis focus on understanding and extracting meaning from short, informal pieces of text — like tweets, SMS, headlines, reviews, or chat messages.

What is Micro-text?

Micro-text refers to short-form content, typically:

<280 characters (e.g., tweets, SMS)

Often unstructured, informal, and noisy

Includes slang, abbreviations, misspellings, hashtags, emojis, and code-switching

Challenges in Micro-text Analysis

Challenge	**Example**
Short context	"LOL that's wild 😭"
Spelling variations	"gr8", "gonna", "tmrw"
Hashtags and mentions	"#blessed @user"
Emojis and emoticons	😂, 🤔, :-/
Multilingual content	"Estoy chillin' rn"
Lack of grammar	"me late af"

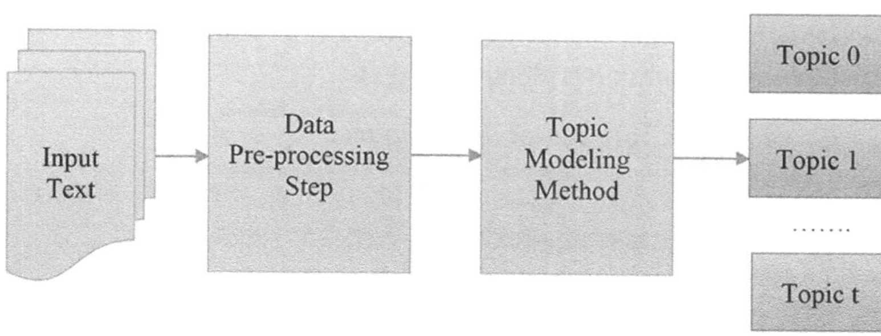

1. Text Preprocessing:

- Tokenization: Breaking down the text into individual words or phrases (tokens).
- Normalization: Converting text to a standard form (e.g., lowercasing, removing punctuation).

- Stemming/Lemmatization: Reducing words to their root form (e.g., "running" to "run").
- Stop word removal: Eliminating common words (like "the," "a," "is") that don't carry much meaning.
- Handling URLs, hashtags, and emoticons: Removing or converting these elements to improve analysis.

2. Syntactic Analysis:

- Part-of-Speech (POS) Tagging: Identifying the grammatical role of each word (noun, verb, adjective, etc.).
- Chunking: Grouping adjacent words into meaningful phrases (e.g., noun phrases, verb phrases).
- Parsing: Analyzing the grammatical structure of sentences.

3. Semantic Analysis:

- Sentiment Analysis: Determining the emotional tone of the text (positive, negative, neutral).
- Named Entity Recognition (NER): Identifying and classifying named entities like people, organizations, locations, etc.
- Topic Modeling: Discovering underlying themes or topics within a collection of texts.

4. Other Important Techniques:

- Keyword Extraction: Identifying the most important words or phrases in a text.
- Text Summarization: Generating concise summaries of longer texts.
- Machine Translation: Translating text from one language to another.

5. Applications:

- Social Media Analysis: Understanding public opinion, identifying trends, and monitoring brand reputation.
- Customer Feedback Analysis: Extracting insights from customer reviews and feedback.
- Chatbots and Virtual Assistants: Enabling more natural and intelligent conversations.
- Information Retrieval: Improving search results by understanding the context of queries.

Example Application Areas

- Twitter sentiment monitoring
- Spam detection in SMS or chat
- Real-time event detection
- Customer feedback classification
- Chatbot understanding (intent classification)

Toolkits and Libraries

Library	Use Case
NLTK, spaCy	Basic NLP tasks
emoji, emot	Emoji interpretation
VADER, TextBlob	Rule-based sentiment analysis
Hugging Face	Transformer-based models
CMU ARK Tools	Twitter POS/NER/sentiment
BERTopic	Topic modeling from micro-texts

5.16 Trend

A trend is a general direction in which something is developing or changing over time. In various contexts, the meaning and method of detecting trends can differ slightly.

Types of Trends by Domain

1. Data Science / Analytics

Definition: A pattern of change in data over time (upward, downward, cyclical).

Example: Increasing customer churn over 6 months.

Detection: Time series analysis (e.g., moving averages, regression, ARIMA).

2. Social Media

Definition: A topic, hashtag, or meme that gains rapid popularity.

Example: #Barbenheimer, viral TikTok audio.

Detection: High frequency of mentions or shares in a short time span.

3. Business & Marketing

Definition: A shift in consumer behavior or market dynamics.

Example: Rise of plant-based diets, remote work tools.

Detection: Market research, surveys, social listening, sales data.

4. Fashion & Culture

Definition: A popular style or behavior that spreads widely.

Example: Vintage Y2K fashion comeback, slang like "rizz".

Detection: Observational data, influencer activity, cultural moments.

Tools for Trend Analysis

- Google Trends — search interest over time
- TrendHunter, Exploding Topics — upcoming consumer trends

- Hootsuite / Brandwatch — social media trend monitoring
- Twitter API — real-time trending topics
- Tableau / Power BI — visual analytics tools
- Python Libraries:
- pandas, matplotlib, seaborn — time series plots
- Prophet, ARIMA — forecasting trends
- tweepy, snscrape — scraping social data

5.17 Social influencers on judgments

Social influencers—whether people, media figures, or even peers—can strongly impact our judgments and decision-making processes. This influence can be conscious or unconscious, and it's widely studied in psychology, marketing, behavioral economics, and social media research.

Who Are Social Influencers?

- ❖ Celebrities
- ❖ Social media influencers
- ❖ Friends or family
- ❖ Experts or thought leaders
- ❖ Online reviewers and content creators

How Do Social Influencers Shape Judgments?

1. Social Proof

People assume the actions of others reflect correct behavior.

Example: Seeing thousands of likes on a post makes people more likely to trust the content or product.

2. Authority Bias

We are more likely to trust and follow judgments made by experts or figures in authority.

Example: Following medical advice from a famous doctor on Instagram, even without verifying credentials.

3. Bandwagon Effect

Judgments shift because "everyone else is doing it."

Example: Choosing a restaurant that's trending on TikTok, even if reviews are mixed.

4. Halo Effect

A positive impression in one area (e.g., attractiveness, popularity) influences opinions in another.

Example: Trusting a fitness influencer's financial advice based on their charisma or lifestyle.

5. Mere Exposure Effect

Repeated exposure increases familiarity and likability—even if objective quality is low.

Example: A song feels "better" after hearing it many times through an influencer's content.

6. Framing and Persuasion

Influencers often frame decisions in emotionally persuasive ways.

- "You NEED this in your life 💯"
- "I was skeptical too, but this changed everything…"

5.17 Opinion spread

Opinion spread refers to how beliefs, ideas, attitudes, or preferences propagate through a group of individuals—especially in social networks, both online and offline. It's a key concept in social psychology, network science, marketing, and computational sociology.

How Opinions Spread

Opinions can spread much like viruses in epidemiology, memes in culture, or rumors online.

Mechanism	Description
Contagion Model	People "catch" opinions from others they interact with (e.g., word of mouth, retweets).
Threshold Model	A person adopts an opinion when enough of their peers already hold it.
Cascade Model	A small seed of influential people starts a chain reaction.
Echo Chambers	People mostly interact with like-minded individuals, reinforcing shared opinions.

Factors Influencing Opinion Spread

1. Influencer Centrality

Highly connected or respected individuals (e.g., social media influencers) can trigger widespread diffusion.

2. Network Topology

Dense, clustered networks can spread ideas quickly within a group.

Sparse or disconnected networks slow diffusion.

3. Reinforcement & Repetition

Opinions seen multiple times (via retweets or reposts) are more likely to be accepted (mere exposure effect).

4. Homophily (Birds of a Feather)

People are more likely to adopt opinions from similar others (friends, same political views, etc.).

5. Content Framing

Emotionally charged or simply framed opinions (e.g., memes or slogans) tend to spread faster.

Opinion Spread in Social Media

Platform	Opinion Spreading Mechanisms
Twitter	Retweets, hashtags, trending topics
Facebook	Comments, reactions, shares
Reddit	Upvotes/downvotes, subreddit virality
TikTok	Audio trends, duets, influencer reposts

Real-World Applications

- Marketing: Spreading product opinions or reviews.
- Elections: Shaping voter perceptions.
- Public Health: Spreading vaccine hesitancy or support.
- Misinformation: How fake news goes viral.

Numerical Problem: Opinion Spread in a Social Network

Problem Statement: You have a network of 100 people. Initially, 5 people hold a specific opinion (e.g., support for a product). Each person can influence 3 others per day.

Assume:

Every person who adopts the opinion will try to influence others the next day.

There's a 30% probability that a contact adopts the opinion.

Once influenced or exposed, people don't revert or get influenced again.

Q1: How many people will hold the opinion after 3 days, assuming no duplicate targeting and no repeat influence.?

Step-by-Step Solution

Day 0 (Initial State)

Opinion holders: 5

Day 1

Each of the 5 people tries to influence 3 people → $5 \times 3 = 15$ people contacted

Each contact has a 30% chance of adopting the opinion

→ Expected new opinion holders = $15 \times 0.3 = 4.5 \approx 5$ people

Cumulative total: 5 (original) + 5 = 10

Day 2

Now 10 people hold the opinion → $10 \times 3 = 30$ contacts

Expected new holders: $30 \times 0.3 = 9$

Cumulative total: $10 + 9 = 19$

Day 3

19 people hold the opinion → $19 \times 3 = 57$ contacts

Expected new holders: $57 \times 0.3 = 17.1 \approx 17$

Cumulative total: $19 + 17 = 36$

5.18 Judgement

Judgment is the cognitive process of forming an opinion, evaluation, or conclusion based on available information, experience, and reasoning.

Points About Judgment

- Involves assessment: We evaluate facts, evidence, or situations.
- Basis for decisions: Judgments guide choices and actions.
- Can be biased: Influenced by emotions, heuristics, social factors, and cognitive biases.

Types:

- Moral judgment: Deciding right vs. wrong.
- Risk judgment: Estimating probability and impact of events.
- Social judgment: Evaluating others' behavior or intentions.

Example in Practice

- Medical diagnosis: Doctor judges symptoms and test results to conclude a diagnosis.
- Consumer behavior: Buyer judges product quality based on reviews and brand reputation.

References:

1. Matthew Ganis, Avinash Kohirkar, Social Media Analytics: Techniques and Insights for Extracting Business Value Out of Social Media Pearson 2016
2. Jim Sterne, Social Media Metrics: How to Measure and Optimize Your Marketing Investment Wiley Latest edition
3. Brian Clifton, Advanced Web Metrics with Google Analytics, John Wiley & Sons; 3rd Edition edition (30 Mar 2012)
4. Ganis/Kohirka, SOCIAL MEDIAANALYTICS Paperback – 29 September 2016 by Pearson.